CLIVE PEARSON

E.G. Clark
1997

CLIVE PEARSON

A LIFE

1887–1965

JOHN JOLLIFFE

MICHAEL RUSSELL

© John Jolliffe 1992

First published in Great Britain 1992
by Michael Russell (Publishing) Ltd
Wilby Hall, Wilby, Norwich NR16 2JP

Typeset at The Spartan Press Limited
Lymington, Hampshire
Printed and bound in Great Britain
by Biddles Ltd, Guildford and King's Lynn

All rights reserved
ISBN 0 85955 184 9

Contents

	Preface	7
1	Early Background and Education	11
2	Early Work, the War and Marriage	20
3	Parham and Castle Fraser	32
4	Chile	51
5	Life between the Wars	65
6	Collecting Pictures and Books	80
7	Aircraft Companies and BOAC	92
8	The War at Home	107
9	Last Years	116
	APPENDIX A: The Library at Parham by Nicholas Poole-Wilson	130
	APPENDIX B: House of Lords Debate on BOAC (from *Hansard*)	135
	Index	151

Preface

This book has been written at the request of Clive Pearson's three daughters: Veronica, Mrs P. H. Tritton, to whom I am extremely grateful for endless hospitality when I was working on the files at Parham; Lavinia, Mrs Michael Smiley, who kindly entertained me at Castle Fraser and assisted greatly over the illustrations, but who very sadly died before seeing the book in print, as did her husband; and Dione, Lady Gibson, who with Lord Gibson has also given me invaluable help. Lavinia's daughter Miranda, the Countess of Iveagh, has been equally patient and helpful with all kinds of inquiries.

Their cheerful recommendation to 'leave out the dull bits' has sometimes been harder to follow than they may have imagined, partly because of the equal danger of missing out, or failing to establish, the interesting bits. Any defects that there may be in the book have not arisen through lack of materials. When Clive Pearson (hereafter referred to for clarity, but not altogether appropriately, as Clive) retired in 1957, he took with him to Parham thirty-seven files relating to the family estates in Sussex, and to polo, hunting, and other local activities; and fifteen parcels, each containing up to eight files and notebooks, also chiefly concerned with the family businesses. There are also at Parham fifty-three box files covering household accounts, correspondence with his architect and friend Victor Heal, sailing activities, accounts from a wide range of dealers in pictures and books, and other subjects including shooting, stockbreeding, and the Lady Zouche Parham Nursing Bequest. Apart from these personal records, a further seventy box files were deposited in the Library of the Museum of Science and Industry when Pearsons moved their office from Parliament Street to less spacious premises at Millbank Tower. They contain records of S. Pearson & Son, Whitehall Securities, Whitehall Electric, the Cowdray Trust, British Airways, and many individual companies. From this mountain of material I have done my best to avoid producing an interminable and unreadable history of the Pearson Group in all its ramifications, but to concentrate on summarising

Clive's own activities in business, as a family man, and as the owner of three large houses and three country estates. Each owes a great deal of its character to his own work in managing it and to the example that he set. But here too I have tried not to bury the reader under a mass of detail. At this distance of time, the tariff rates for the electricity used by the Santiago Tramways in 1927 may appear very similar to those for 1926, crucial though the difference was at the time. The same applies to the fatstock prices and their fluctuations at Aberdeen in the 1930s.

There were however some disappointing gaps in the materials. First, very few of the letters that must have been exchanged between Clive and his phenomenal father have survived. Secondly, Clive preserved no record of the major part that he and his brother played in the salvation of Lazards in its crisis in 1931, which must have been one of the two or three most important achievements of his business career. Thirdly, no trace has survived of how he commissioned Evelyn Waugh to write *Robbery under Law*, the somewhat distorted picture of Mexico at the time of the expropriation of foreign-owned assets by the Cardenas government in 1938. Nor have any letters survived from Clive to his wife.

I should like to thank Viscount Cowdray, who not only began his work in the family group under Clive's guidance but is also the last survivor of his board of directors; His nephew Lord Cranworth gave me a clear impression of how kindly and hospitable Clive was to younger members of the family, and his secretary Miss M. M. Tewkesbury has also been of special help in tracing the later history of the Amerada and Rycade companies after Clive's own records of them cease. As regards BOAC, the late Lord Runciman helped me only a few weeks before his death with some trenchant observations about the corporation, and I am also grateful in that field to Sir Ross Stainton, Mr Alan Campbell Orde, his stepdaughter Mrs Haynes, and above all to Sir Robert Maxwell. Mr David Pawson kindly gave me some first-hand information about the Athens Piraeus Company. Turning to matters at home, Mr Alan Hughes, who worked as agent at Paddockhurst to Clive, and later to the Trittons, and Mr Gordon Duke, Clive's chief farm manager at Parham, both gave me vivid impressions of what it was like to work for him, as did his secretary Miss Rosemary Courcier, whose loyal and affectionate tributes to him are of unique significance. Lord Egremont gave me a good story about his family's relations with the Pearsons. Mrs Rosemary Goff, the daughter of Clive's old friend Toby Fitzwilliam, has kindly provided photographs from her albums as well as answering various questions in a particularly helpful and friendly way, for which I am especially grateful. Mrs Jeanne Bennett, the daughter of Victor Heal, also helped me with a number of details; and my thanks are also due to Mrs Pat Kennedy, the administrator at Parham, and Mrs Pam Dubreil, Veronica Tritton's secretary.

On a visit to Chile I was given help and hospitality by the following, which transformed what would otherwise have been a lonely and difficult business: Mr and Mrs Richard Lavers of the British Embassy; Professor Julio Retamal and Dr Ricardo Couyoumdjian of the Catholic University of Santiago; Mr Agostin Edwards and Don Jaime Antunez Aldunate of *El Mercurio*; Don Fernando Bravo of Chilectra; Donna Lucia Santa Cruz de Ossa; Mr and Mrs Stephen Drysdale, whose help and hospitality was exceptionally generous; Count and Countess Rule von Bismarck; Donna Nena Ossa, at that time Director of the Museo de Bellas Artes in Santiago; Mr Richard Cheney of Cimento Melon; Admiral Lemay and Captain and Mrs Kenneth Pugh at Valparaiso. I also benefited from various glimpses of the invigorating company at that haven for any biographer, the Café del Biografo.

I am also grateful to H. E. Don Bernardo Sepolveda, the current Mexican Ambassador in London, for his guidance over the expropriation of foreign assets in Mexico in 1938. Mr Nicholas Poole-Wilson of Quaritch kindly helped me with information, not otherwise available, about the formation of the great collection of books at Parham.

It is hardly necessary to add finally that any errors of fact or emphasis that may be found in what follows are not to be blamed on those who have so kindly provided information, but are my own responsibility.

I
Early Background and Education

Clive Pearson was born on 12 August 1887, the third child and second son of Weetman Pearson, afterwards 1st Viscount Cowdray, and his wife Annie Cass, whose father Sir John Cass was at one time Lord Mayor of Bradford. The family firm of contractors, S. Pearson & Son, had been based in Bradford since 1844, and had by this time established an important reputation by completing a series of massive public works which included the Sheffield main sewer, the harbour at King's Lynn, the docks at Halifax, Nova Scotia and the Empress Dock at Southampton. In the course of Clive's childhood the firm would become the biggest contractors in the world, as a result of undertaking – among many other lesser projects – the building of the Blackwall Tunnel, the Admiralty Harbour at Dover, the Tehuantepec Railway in Mexico, the ports at each end of it, and the Sennar Dam on the Blue Nile.

The story of Weetman Pearson's triumphant career has been vividly told in *Member for Mexico* by Desmond Young (Cassell, 1966) but it is worth recording that apart from his business career, and his almost uncanny powers of accurate estimating of contracts, he was a devoted husband whose marriage partnership was quite unusually successful and harmonious. Annie Pearson was an exceptionally purposeful and capable woman, and if her ideas on the life style appropriate for her husband and herself (and her rigid views on the kind of husband she wanted for her daughter) may seem excessively worldly today, the context of the late Victorian and Edwardian eras has to be borne in mind. The Pearsons had reached the top of the tree, financially and socially, and it seemed right and proper that the fact should be recognised. No shadow of egalitarianism ever crossed the sunlit plateau to which they had ascended as a result of their own intensely hard work, powerful intelligence and prodigious commercial success. But a particularly attractive aspect of Weetman Pearson's character is shown by a later episode after his firm had constructed the East River Tunnels in New York. The verdict on this achievement in the *Wall Street Journal* was that it was 'perhaps a little bit hard on the pride of the Americans in their self-asserted leadership in "enterprise" that the greatest engineering undertaking in the history of this country is being carried out by a firm of Englishmen'. A few years later Pearson found himself next to an American matron at dinner in London, who enlarged on the superiority of American engineers over all others and mentioned the East River Tunnels as a crowning example of their skill and enterprise. In the words of his official biographer, 'Pearson gravely promised her that he would not omit to visit them and examine them carefully when he was next in New York'.

On the other hand, people were sometimes in awe of him, even as a young man. A Yorkshire bank manager is said to have told a subordinate 'When you see young Pearson coming, give me time to get under the counter.' And once the Pearsons had established their commanding position, false modesty never reared its head. After a particularly arduous and uncomfortable spell in Mexico, they had once spent a few days recuperating in New York. Mrs Pearson was presented with a solid silver bicycle from the window of Tiffany's by her husband, in gratitude for the perfect care she took of him. Nor was it shut up in a glass case. It was used by its owner, and is still in working order at Dunecht. It was an age when material success, especially if hard-earned, was looked up to without reservation as something to be proud of; and in the Pearsons' case, it was undeniably justified by their liberal-minded attitude to their employees, and in due course by public benefactions on a huge scale, amounting to many millions of pounds in today's money.

Clive inherited his father's meticulous methods to the full, and later in his life new colleagues, such as the directors of Imperial Airways who worked with him in what had become BOAC in the Second World War, were sometimes antagonised by what they regarded as an excessive attention to detail at a time when large issues were at stake and great decisions had to be taken at speed. But in his early business life, in the Anglo-Mexican oil companies, he was working within the broad outlines of an existing policy, and day-to-day detail was all-important. Good habits, acquired early, are not easily shaken off. His approach would be the same when it came to handling the opportunities and problems at Parham. Clive would never go in for stupendous risks, as his father had done in the rebuilding of the railway across the Mexican isthmus and the construction of a large port at each end. His father had been the originator of these massive schemes; his own task was to consolidate them, and then to advance logically in new directions, but without taking comparable steps in the dark. As will be seen, he later had to cope with the unfamiliar and hazardous circumstances of the Wall Street crash and the slump. Great businesses were to go bankrupt right and left, and unemployment on an unprecedented scale would follow. It would be a context that called for a different outlook, and often different skills, from the ones which his father had so successfully developed. But what was common to them both was attention to detail, and the willingness to examine each problem as it arose from a large number of angles in rapid succession before calmly deciding on a course of action.

Clive was born at 16 Airlie Gardens, a large modern house in a solid, respectable part of Kensington, at the top of Campden Hill. His mother had furnished the first London office which S. Pearson & Son had established, in Westminster, and she and her husband spent Saturday afternoons working in it together, after the staff had left. The office had soon been moved to 10 Victoria Street, a significant step up in the business world, but Weetman Pearson still did most of the work himself. (Desmond Young has recorded that for eight years he never took a holiday, and when bank holidays came round, he stayed in bed and slept through them to restore his energies.) When Clive was seven, his father was made a baronet, and also acquired Paddockhurst, an already spacious country house near Crawley in Sussex, much of which he rebuilt on an even larger scale, together with an estate of 3,000 acres. Later, having bought various other country properties, he generously offered Paddockhurst as a temporary base to his friend Porfirio Diaz, the President of Mexico, on his fall from power and exile in 1911. This was to be the centre of extensive entertaining, and the background of Clive's family holidays from school and university. Before the days of antiseptics and antibiotics, country air was more than a pleasant change, it was a good deal healthier than the smoke and fogs of London, and was correspondingly even more sought after by those who could afford it than it is today. Four years later, the family again moved house in London to the palatial surroundings of 16 Carlton House Terrace, where their neighbours would include the Duke of Devonshire, Lord Curzon and Lord Northcliffe. It was not only an imposing house outside, but it had been modified between 1863 and 1866 by the entrepreneur Sir Samuel Morton Peto, and contains modelled ceilings in polychrome, with much gilding as well, and elaborate panelling on the walls in rare and costly woods. In 1899 Clive's father drew up, in his own hand, for the benefit of his twelve-year-old son, the following list of contracts on which the company was engaged, with his own comments on them.

CONTRACTS THAT W. D. PEARSON IS CARRYING OUT, NOVEMBER 1899

Name of Contract	Manager	Amount of Contract	No. of men employed
Admiralty Harbour, Dover	K. Macdonald	£3,300,000	2,000
Granite Works (quarry), Cornwall	E. E. Pearson	—	400
Cement Works, London	E. E. Pearson	—	400
East London Waterworks, London	E. E. Pearson	300,000	1,000
Surrey Commercial Dock, London	E. W. Moir	400,000	1,000
Great Northern and City Railway, London	E. W. Moir	2,000,000	1,500
Seaham Harbour Company, Durham	T. L. Walsh	350,000	1,000
Great Western Railway, Gloucestershire	G. Hay	1,000,000	3,000
Port Talbot Docks, South Wales	J. Davies	—	200
Vera Cruz Harbour, Mexico	J. B. Body	2,000,000	4,000
Main Drainage, Dublin	B. C. Cass	100,000	500
Ross and Wicklow Railway, Ireland	F. T. Hopkinson	100,000	500
Tehuantepec Railway, Mexico	J. B. Body	2,500,000	4,000
Railways in China	—	—	—

Besides the above, we have other contracts that are not at present ready to start but which require watching and thinking about.

(Signed) W. D. PEARSON

MEMO. PREPARED FOR CLIVE PEARSON
Remarks

Breakwaters to enclose 1 square mile of deep water. A Harbour of safety for H.M. ships. The walls of Breakwaters are 60 ft. thick and 80 ft. high. Work difficult. Contract time 9 years.

This quarry was bought to supply Dover with the granite facing required for the concrete blocks, with which the breakwaters are built and which weigh from 20 to 40 tons each.

These works were bought to supply Dover and our other contracts with cement. They are being extended so as to make 2,000 tons of Portland Cement a week.

The contract is to construct 2 Reservoirs to store water in winter ready for use in summer. They are about as large as our park at Paddockhurst. They supply East London with water.

We are here making an old dock, built 100 years ago, into a modern one. The size of ships has so largely increased that old docks are useless.

This is a railway 3 miles long, all underground, running from Finsbury Park Station to the City (Moorgate Street). It is lined with iron plates instead of brick.

This is a new harbour and also making an old dock into a new one for the Marquess of Londonderry, who requires them to load his coal into ships.

This is a very heavy railway. There is a tunnel 2½ miles long and a short one, besides 3 heavy viaducts. There are 47 locomotives being used. This runs through Badminton.

This is nearly finished after 4 years' work. The docks are required for the shipment of coal, to foreign ports principally. They can load a 2,000-ton ship in 1 day.

This is a large harbour for the Mexican Government, and is now probably the best harbour in North America. Have been at work 4 years, and will take 2 to finish.

This is a contract that B. got and is just starting. It is for the outfall works of the sewers of Dublin and is a very pretty job.

A railway some 12 or 16 miles long, I forget which, of no particular difficulty or importance.

This is the lease of a railway 200 miles long between the Atlantic and Pacific Oceans and also for the construction of 2 ports. The lease is for 50 years and is by far the most serious business we have ever undertaken. If I had nothing else to do I should be busy on this alone.

This contract is all settled, but the Company are not yet ready to start operations. They will be this year, when we begin the making of some 200 or more miles of railway.

It will be seen that Clive and his wife were later to react against the rather formal magnificence with which his mother, in the spirit of the success stories of the times, had surrounded her family. They certainly accumulated great treasures at Parham, but as will be seen their first concern was to preserve the atmosphere of a fine old house, instead of creating something new. But already in 1898 Clive's father had evidently decided that he was to play a major role in running the business that had made all this possible.

Money may have been the symbol of their success, but in Sir Weetman's code it had to be made by hard work resulting in a tangible end product, and not by canny investment in other people's businesses. He is said to have warned his daughter Gertrude, 'Never marry a stockbroker. Those people have no standard.'

Few details of Clive's childhood survive, but in his last year at Cambridge a light-hearted article appeared in the magazine *Granta* in a series with the tongue-in-cheek title of *Those in Authority*. It includes the following passage, how accurate it is hard to say: 'In the absence of his elders he used to organise great nursery hunts . . . neatly attired in a pink sash, with a little tin trumpet cunningly stuck in the frills of his bib, and magnificently mounted on a weight-carrying rocking-horse.' (The rocking-horse survives in perfect condition to this day in the Long Gallery at Parham.) He was sent to a preparatory school at Eastbourne called St Christopher's, where he seems to have been happy, or at any rate uncomplaining. Indeed his praise for the food and the comfort of the beds in his letters home makes rather surprising reading. He could write out the Greek alphabet by the time he was ten and his reports were reasonably favourable, though there are references to dreaminess and inattention. When he went on to Rugby in 1898, his reports mention 'very good work' in classics, and describe him as 'very satisfactory all round, always anxious to understand things thoroughly, but apt to create unnecessary difficulties for himself, and to become obstinate over them'. By the summer of 1901, however, he 'might do better in work'. Next year he is described as 'well meaning, but casual in everything he does. Always pleasant but not always reliable.' And in the winter of 1902 'generally rather disappointing', and 'just needs more energy'. In later life he would recall no particularly happy memories of Rugby, which must have been a bleak enough place at the time. His letters home however are generally cheerful, perhaps because he felt that that was what his mother wished to hear; but they are not revealing enough to be worth quoting.

Part of the summer holidays of 1904 was spent touring Normandy by motor-cycle in the company of a young clergyman called John Robins, selected no doubt by Clive's mother. Clive found him a congenial companion, there were many breakdowns and punctures, but also enjoyable visits to Bayeux, Caen, Honfleur, and Coutances. After one more term he left Rugby a few months after his seventeenth birthday and spent the first few months of 1905 in Mexico, gaining his first impressions of the family firm in action. It is interesting to compare this tour with his father's first venture abroad. The young Weetman Pearson had been packed off to America alone, on his nineteenth birthday, as a second-class passenger, on a four-month tour. He was given a roving commission to keep his eyes open for business, especially in possible markets for the bricks, glazed tiles and sanitary pipes which were at that time manufactured by the family firm in Bradford, and were an important source of its income. By the time of Clive's first visit to Mexico, the family firm had come a long way. He presented the President's beautiful second wife, Carmen Diaz, with a book of photographs, to which she responded enthusiastically, addressing him as 'Muy apreciable Clive', expressing 'un milion de gracias' and telling him that the pictures were 'muy bonitas y perfectamente tornadas'. (Clive's father had incidentally given the first dredger used in the harbour works at Vera Cruz the name of *Carmen*, and had also tactfully given the name Carmen Junction to a station on the Tehuantepec Railway, rather after the fashion of Victoria Station in London.)

It seems strange nowadays, but was typical of the attitudes of the time, that in spite of his close early contacts with Mexico – and also with Chile where he was later to buy a house of his own – Clive never learnt Spanish, but relied, like his father, on colleagues and interpreters.

Clive's elder brother Harold was married in November 1905, to a niece of the Duke of Marlborough. They were given a large house on the Cowdray estate, and the rest of the family tended to use Cowdray Park in the summer and Paddockhurst in the winter. The rest of the family thereafter were based at Paddockhurst. Clive went up to Trinity College, Cambridge in the autumn, and by the next year was playing polo for the University, having also begun to win steeplechases on his horses Eve May and Chorister. The sporting life was evidently led at some cost to his work. Adam Sedgwick, the Professor of Zoology and Senior Tutor in Natural Sciences, calmly informed him that in the examination at the end of his first year he had only scored 160 marks out of 560, 200 being the minimum for a third class pass. 'Your Director of Studies says you may go on with the Tripos work but there will of course be a certain risk of your being thrown out next year. But I think it is worth the risk if you are willing to work this vacation and are not afraid to work next year.' Clive evidently heeded this warning, since as well as winning more steeplechases and polo matches he graduated with a degree in mechanical sciences in 1908, to the enthusiastic applause of his parents. A letter from his father survives, dated October 1907, which is in splendid contrast to those of most fathers to their undergraduate sons. It offered Clive, who had broken his collar-bone, a motor-car to the value of £500 or £600, with a man to act as chauffeur and valet, and an extra £100 a year for running expenses. 'If you think', it went on, 'my views are not too extravagant then we can act on them without the necessity of a talk.' In May 1908, before Clive's final examination, his father wrote again: 'Do not work too hard, to feel fagged for your exam. So long as we know you have worked and worked hard, whether you score as you hope or not will not materially matter.' On 15 June, when the results were known, his mother wrote in her characteristic style: 'When your wire was phoned through the earth was full of joy but we nearly walked on air, we were so pleased and proud.' He had got a third.

He had already joined the Sussex Yeomanry, as was expected of the sons of prominent local landowners, and his twenty-first birthday fell in August while he was in camp with them. He received another letter from his mother, saying that 'I am of course very disappointed we are not with you for the day, but as on duty for your country I bow always to what is right . . . I look for a few selfish years at least with you at home with me.' A more relaxed note was struck by his elder sister Gertrude, known as 'Trudie', with whom he was always on the warmest terms, and who wrote 'You seem so very old only to be just coming of age.'

Clive stayed up at Cambridge another year, as *Granta* put it, 'to wrestle with the intricacies of bookkeeping – once a fortnight – which leaves him ample leisure for the more serious pursuits of life . . . He is essentially a sportsman and a good fellow, and singularly lacking in self-assertiveness.' His father was still Member of Parliament for Colchester, and Clive attended the Colchester Oyster Feast in October, a sumptuous civic affair at which his father proposed the toast of the armed forces, seconded by General Baden-Powell, the founder of the Boy Scouts. The Japanese Ambassador was the principal guest, and for some reason the Duke of Marlborough proposed the toast of 'The Drama'. In 1910, when his father took a peerage, Clive was sounded out to see if he would consider being nominated as Liberal candidate, but politics seem to have had little appeal for him at any time and he was able to decline on the grounds that he expected to be abroad on business for some months. In the same month as the Feast, he was given his first direct impression of one of his father's major achievements when he attended the opening of the new Admiralty Harbour at Dover. Its existence was to be of incalculable value when war came in 1914, and effectively prevented the German High Fleet from ever putting to sea after the Battle of Jutland, or of having access to the English Channel.

Apart from the general camaraderie of equestrian sport, his nature was plainly reserved, and he remained in some ways a shy man to the end of his life. He seems to have made very few close or lasting friendships at Cambridge except with Toby Fitzwilliam, afterwards a neighbour in Sussex. Being of a historical as well as a sporting turn of mind, he was to help Clive later on by compiling, in scholarly fashion, the collection of documents entitled *Parham in Sussex*. Clive, in return, helped him at more than one crisis, was best man at his wedding, and as will be seen they remained life-long friends.

2
Early Work, the War and Marriage

When Clive came down from Cambridge in 1909, having presumably mastered at least some of the intricacies of bookkeeping referred to in *Granta*, it was to plunge into the operations of the family companies and to experience at first hand what he had already heard so much about from his father. Following the discovery of oil on land controlled by the company at Pedregal as far back as 1901, Weetman Pearson had quickly acquired concessions over vast areas, and in the following year told J. A. Spender, later editor of the *Westminster Gazette* and eventually his official biographer, that he intended to put a million and a half of his money into oil, no more and no less. By 1912, one thing had led to another, and he had invested no less than £5m of his own and the firm's money. What had brought about this vast increase of scale?

In 1901 the Waters Pierce Oil Co., owned one third by Henry Clay Pierce and two thirds by Standard Oil of New Jersey, had long had the monopoly of the retail oil trade in Mexico, which extended to 700 barrels of oil a day. But the fact that it was able to charge a price which was publicly regarded as excessive gave Weetman Pearson his chance. As Spender explains, 'As a producer of oil in Mexico he might have been welcome, for Waters Pierce were not themselves producers, and were actually in need of oil produced on the spot, to avoid the freight and duty costs of importing it.' But since he decided from the start to be a distributor as well as a producer he was an obvious threat to the monopolist. By April 1907 he had convinced himself that he would find oil in sufficient quantities to justify a refinery and a distribution network. For the past four years he had been willing to come to a deal of some kind with Pierce, but this having proved abortive he finally decided in 1908 to go into action as a retailer in Mexico, having entered into an agreement with C. T. Bowring & Co., a large firm of oil distributors in England (soon amalgamated with Pearson's) to buy the products of his Mexican refinery at Minatitlan. In view of all this, there could hardly have been a more crucial or exciting moment for Clive to be joining the firm, and just before the opening of the refinery in March 1908, Sir Weetman embarked on a long letter from Mexico to Clive, still at Cambridge, which he never posted, or even finished, but retained among his papers. The pressure of his work and the scale of his operations had never been greater, and the fact that he found time to start writing it (though it may have been partly to calm his own mind) must also indicate that he had already settled that Clive was to play a big part in the business very soon.

I find things about as I expected [he wrote]. The San Cristobal oilfield only gives us two years' life; *but surely before that two years has passed we shall have found further deposits of a satisfactory quality* . . . The one encouraging feature about the oilfield is that one well has continued to flow about 100 tons a day for 10 or 12 weeks . . . we may have a much more lasting field than the depths of oil-bearing rocks and sands have led me to believe. As you know, we hedged by agreeing to purchase from Furbero a minimum of 2,000 and a maximum of 6,000 barrels a day for twelve years (to feed the new refinery). So if we do fail to find more oil (an almost unimaginable assumption) we avoid a failure. All this you know already, *but it is cheering to put it down on paper when disappointments are all around me.*

Much detail should hour by hour be gone into to avoid all waste. Everyone, on an oilfield, is naturally inclined to be extremely wasteful, as it is considered to lead to untold wealth. And beyond all it is essential to know the business, *otherwise the opinions of one's employees have to prevail.* I entered lightly into the enterprise, not realising its many problems, but only feeling that oil meant a fortune and that hard work and application would bring satisfactory results. Now I know that it would have been wise to surround myself with proved oil men . . . However I feel we are out of the wood, and should we have plenty of oil on our hands we have a great business, one that my sons will be proud of.

In July of that year Sir Weetman effectively declared war on Waters Pierce by entering into competition with them in the retailing business in Mexico itself. He ordered forty tank cars to distribute oil to the chief commercial centres in the country, then began establishing depots, first at fifteen principal centres, increased by the end of 1909 to 160. By 1910 he could claim to be selling half of the refined burning oil in Mexico and nearly a quarter of the lubricating oil. But he was still not sure of his supplies. A tantalising drama had unfolded in June 1908. The Dos Bocas well in the San Diego field in Northern Vera Cruz began to flow, but then it caught fire and burned for eight weeks, the flames sometimes reaching a height of 500 feet. A million tons of oil were destroyed, worth £1m, and the firm, with the help of the British Ambassador Sir Thomas Hohler, had to compensate local landowners whose property had been laid waste. It says a lot for Pearson's reputation that it was so little damaged by what must have been an appalling disaster for the entire local population. A lesser man would have been discouraged, but Sir Weetman took the cheerful view that if one well could produce £1m worth of oil, others could too. Meanwhile, however, he was buying oil from Texas and the Furbero field in Mexico and selling it at a considerable loss, giving all concerned a time of acute anxiety. By January 1910 his optimism was rewarded by the discovery of new wells between Vera Cruz and Tampico, territory where he had only acquired concessions with some reluctance. Following on the first wells in the Potrero field, and another thirty miles north of Tuxpam (and only 115 feet below ground) he launched the Aguila, or Mexican Eagle, Oil Co., with a capital of 30 million Mexican dollars, publicly issued.

The chairman was the governor of the local federal district and Pearson was joined on the board by President Diaz' son Porfirio, together with the son-in-law of the owner of 17 million acres of land in Chihuahua. All this flattered Mexican pride, and also created a national interest in upholding the rights on which the British development of public land rested. On the other hand, the American companies which had been slower off the mark in Mexico were jealous of the fact that Mexican Eagle could claim to be an all-Mexican enterprise, free from foreign influence and not dependent on the goodwill of any competitor but only on that of the Mexican public, whose interests it had already served by breaking the previous monopoly and lowering the price of oil to local consumers.

Two days after Christmas the famous Potrero No. 4 well was struck, and flowed uncontrollably at the rate of 100,000 barrels a day for sixty days. Then, through the heroic efforts of the engineers, working in a blinding deluge of oil and suffocating gases, a special appliance known as the Bell nipple was fixed to the well and the flow was brought under control. Most of the oil ran down the Buena Vista river and caught fire between ten and fifteen miles downstream; but a reservoir was created to hold back three million barrels, and work pressed on, night and day, to complete the pipeline from Potrero to the sea. It was the supreme success of the whole enterprise, but it was rapidly followed by violent civil unrest: in May 1911 the mob in Mexico City was carrying fuel to place round houses in order to set fire to them, and torpedoes were being attached to railway lines. Many were killed or injured, and the files contain numerous references to Lord Cowdray's acute anxiety for the safety of his staff.

No exact record of Clive's movements for this hazardous period has survived, but he certainly accompanied his father from Mexico City to Potrero, and was there during this crucial time. He had set out for Mexico that August, equipped with *Kemp's Engineering Handbook* and a slide-rule, another textbook on bookkeeping and accounts, and another volume on *The Meaning of Money*. He appears from his own rather patchy notebooks, often written up in very primitive conditions, to have been chiefly concerned at first with the workings of the Tehuantepec Railway, built by his father between 1898 and 1906 at a cost of £2.5m. It was handling nearly 700,000 tons of freight in 1909, 856,000 tons in 1910, and 1,028,000 in 1911, as against his father's original projection of 600,000 tons as a satisfactory target. Other enterprises with which he was concerned on this trip were the Tuxpango Calcium Nitrate Plant and the Alvarada Railway, important for freight in a part of the country favourable for sugar growing and cattle raising. He also learnt the details of the activities of the Vera Cruz Light and Power Co., and this prepared him for the business of the Whitehall Electric Co., which was to become one of the linchpins of the post-war Pearson group after the sale of the control of Mexican Eagle. Altogether, the experience he gained was on a broad front. He also seems to have visited Cuba in connection with some unidentified project, and a letter has survived from his father dated 13 March 1914 saying: 'I assume that the cause of your prolonged stay in Cuba arose from the delay in your cable communications with Body [the general manager of Pearson's in Mexico]; or, which I hope may be the case, that you were taking a little holiday . . . I believe your office [at Anglo-Mexican Petroleum Products] is feeling flush with cash for the time being.'

Sir Weetman's exploits since 1890 had brought him first the fullest confidence and later the close personal friendship of Porfirio Diaz, the President of Mexico. In Spender's words, 'the President was convinced that the Englishman could do anything, and saw in him the appointed instrument for the modernisation of Mexico. First at Puebla and then at Vera Cruz, transmission lines were built to the hydro-electric development at Tuxpango Falls, and later the electricity companies at Orizaba and Cordoba were joined on to the new system. In all these operations Clive played his part, involving himself in details ranging from company structure, which was to be changing constantly as turnover grew in the next few years, to analysing the destination of oil products for the home market in Mexico and for shipping to London, Liverpool and Hull. A separate company had been hived off from Mexican Eagle called the

Eagle Oil Transport Co., with initial capital of £1m, which was to own a fleet of tankers planned to number twenty by 1914, and to charter others. Disastrously for him, President Diaz had happened to be in great pain from a septic poisoning of the jaw when Madero's revolutionary movement broke out in May 1911. He resigned the presidency in the same month and a few days later sailed from Vera Cruz for Europe, never to return. His relations with Sir Weetman, now Lord Cowdray, had always been based on complete confidence and trust, which had never been abused in over twenty years. Cowdray offered Diaz his house at Paddockhurst, having himself moved to Cowdray Park, on the edge of Midhurst, about forty miles away, two years before. The President however preferred to settle in Paris, where he later died.

Cowdray wished to behave with his customary correctness to whatever new government should be elected in Mexico, but each one proved in Spender's words to be 'a transient and embarrassed phantom fighting desperately for its life' against fresh waves of revolution.

By 1914 Cowdray had to be dissuaded from going to Mexico because of the danger of his being kidnapped and held to a vast ransom. In 1912 another new company was formed with the name of Anglo-Mexican Petroleum Products, with Clive now as chairman, to act as sole agents to Pearson's for the sale and distribution of oil and petrol. It acquired assets worth £254,000, and in the next year increased its capital to £500,000, with a projected turnover for 1914 of £1,316,000. At the end of 1913 it formalised its relations with Mexican Eagle on the basis that it would buy all the oil produced by Mexican Eagle, and in return the latter should not sell oil to anyone else except for consumption in Mexico and the rest of Central America. AMPP was owned half by Mexican Eagle, and half by Pearson's, and it had the additional function of supplying Mexican Eagle with all the products that it required from outside Mexico. By 1926 Mexican Eagle owned thirty-four tankers, all chartered to AMPP, and though further changes in company structures took place after its acquisition by Shell in 1920, its activities continued successfully until its expropriation by the Mexican government in 1938. But already in 1913, under Clive, AMPP employed no fewer than 800 people, and Mexican Eagle was already producing so much oil by March 1912 that it signed a contract with Standard Oil (now free from its connection with Henry Pierce) to supply 10 million barrels of crude oil within five years, unless prevented by war or other accidents beyond its control. In the same year a contract was entered into with the Admiralty in London which, whether he liked it or not, may well have saved Clive's life, as will be seen. But as well as selling oil for fuel and lubrication in Britain, he was by now busy selling asphalt in Canada, France, Spain and Italy, kerosene to the Deutsche Petroleum Co., and other materials for making and maintaining road surfaces to a number of local authorities in England.

The net profits of Anglo-Mexican Petroleum Products rose steadily in the war years, except for a fall in 1918. They were as follows:

	£		£
1914	51,068	1917	185,665
1915	78,516	1918	180,928
1916	164,450	1919	195,012

Such were Clive's activities and responsibilities in his first years in business, interspersed with polo at Cowdray in the summer, and hunting and shooting in the winter. Under the threat of the European War which many thought they could see coming, he had joined his county Yeomanry regiment, and on the strength of organisational work at its annual camps he had been promoted to the rank of captain by 1914.

When war was declared, the Sussex Yeomanry were called up to a camp near Canterbury, and for the first few months Clive had about one day's leave a week to attend to business. By Christmas the position had become so critical that he wrote to his colonel, the Earl of March, who was his neighbour at Goodwood, explaining his commitments:

We are at present very occupied with Admiralty work: we have an important contract for the supply to the Navy of fuel oil which is shipped from Mexico in our own vessels, while a further large proportion of our tank-steamer fleet is under time or voyage charter to the Admiralty.

To be sure that we live up to our obligations to the full means that the different producing, refining, transport and sales companies must be on top of their work and able to tackle and settle the various problems such as crop up especially when working at high pressure.

For these reasons, and also to some extent because a large number of the office and outdoor staff have enlisted, I should be of service in the City in keeping the organisation together and up to the mark. I have talked to Harold about it and I believe that if I might have leave for three days each week (preferably from Sunday evening to Wednesday evening) I could still keep track of the Squadron clothing equipment pay and rations matters. It would be seldom that I should want to be out of London, and I could get back quickly to Canterbury at any time I might be wanted. I believe I should have no difficulty if it were considered necessary in obtaining a letter from the Admiralty endorsing this application.

The answer came back within a few days:

I really think under the circumstances it would be much better for you to get seconded while your Admiralty work is on. It seems to me that your business is of such an important nature that it would be much best for you to devote your whole time to it instead of tying yourself to three days a week . . . besides which it would really be fairer to the Squadron. We shall all be very sorry to lose you, temporarily . . . if we get sent abroad you would be up against it again . . . you had much better make a good job of the one thing instead of trying to run two shows at once. I am sure no one could do it better than you.

Clive was dismayed. He wrote back on 28 December that he did not like the idea of being seconded if it could possibly be avoided, and that he would like to discuss the matter with his father. Lord Cowdray plainly agreed with the colonel, and wrote in majestic terms to Sir Francis Hopwood at the Admiralty, adding that 'the day by day decisions that have to be taken to minimise the disorganisation resulting from the War really renders his attendance to his two great companies necessary. The position in Mexico further complicates matters and he should be "on the bridge" carefully watching and giving his orders the whole time.' But his usual cheerfulness prevailed, and he also wrote to Clive asking him to tell his brother Harold, who was his squadron commander, that 'I trust his Squadron will not be irretrievably damaged by its prospective loss'. On 6 January W. Graham Greene replied from the Admiralty that the Lords Commissioners would support his application for relief from service with the Sussex Yeomanry. Later in the war, when ignorant recruiting officers twice tried to call him up, he was able to point out that he already held a commission. But after the war he became a life member of the Old Comrades Association of the Yeomanry, and a letter survives from him urging his butler, Cridland, who had served in France, to attend one of its annual dinners. Cridland had originally accompanied Clive to look after his horses at Cambridge, but later became a butler worthy of the golden age of menservants, when Wodehouse created Beach and Jeeves, and when John Christie at Glyndebourne, at the other end of Sussex, chose his butler Childs to be best man at his wedding. If Cridland never quite occupied that position in the course of his progress from Jeeves to Beach, he was always much more than a butler to Clive, and when in the Second War bombs fell near Parham, he went to Clive to complain indignantly, 'That one shook my pantry.'

By 1915 the position of the non-combatant was intensely uncomfortable, and the general atmosphere, as Kitchener's accusing finger pointed down from the recruiting posters, sometimes approached hysteria. Ignorant and self-important observers, seeing the likes of Clive going to an office every day in plain clothes, were all too ready to regard them as shirkers. Letters to Clive from friends on active service all express sympathy, and their general view is expressed by one who wrote that no matter what dangers and hardships surrounded them in action, 'I suppose London is utterly damnable.' His natural reserve has prevented any details about his feelings at the time from surviving, but his wife was later convinced that it had been a severe blow to him to have escaped the lethal danger to which his friends, and particularly his friends in the Yeomanry, were exposed at the front.

These feelings must have been painfully reinforced by the death of his younger brother Geoffrey in action in France, only five weeks after the war began. Geoffrey had succeeded in enlisting among the first of the volunteers, and was acting as a dispatch rider when he lost his way and was captured by a troop of Uhlans. In the course of a British advance soon afterwards, Geoffrey and another prisoner succeeded in escaping, but they were pursued by their captors and Geoffrey was shot dead. He appears to have been a somewhat carefree figure, but in spite of a fundamental difference in temperament Clive was devoted to him. Geoffrey had made a runaway marriage, and for the past two years had been working in one of the family companies in what is now Czechoslovakia. As well as a fair-sized bill from Ladbroke's, and an unsupported claim from an amateur moneylender which Lord Cowdray not surprisingly rejected, Geoffrey also left a baby daughter, who was born at Brno and was summarily adopted by Lady Cowdray; but his widow was afterwards treated in a friendly fashion and attended Clive's own wedding and other family gatherings. Plainly Geoffrey's death not only very much saddened Clive, but brought home to him unpleasantly his own sheltered position.

By the middle of 1915 his staff had indeed melted away. In the products department 42 out of 105 had enlisted, of the Bowrings personnel 22 out of 196, in Transport 7 out of 34, and from Highways 14 out of 36. Many more followed later. But the work went on, and by 1916 no less than 124 depots had been set up all over England for kerosene supplies, and many other spirit stores and tanks. In the quarter to 30 September 1915 261,470 tons of oil products were supplied to the Admiralty, and exports of various kinds continued, including materials for road works in Paris. Some idea of the crucial importance of Clive's work to the war effort may be obtained from the statement by Ludendorff at the end of the war that shortage of oil had been an important reason for the German defeat, and Lord Curzon stated majestically that 'Victory came to us floating on waves of petrol'. In the course of the war, three of the tankers belonging to Eagle Oil Transport were sunk and five more were damaged by torpedoes and later repaired, greatly adding to Clive's responsibilities and the problems that he had to solve. An appetite for work had probably already been ingrained in him by heredity, and it certainly grew as his responsibilities increased, with the added consideration that if he was not to be allowed to fight, he could atone for it by working harder than ever.

Another event occurred in 1915 which was to be of far greater significance to Clive even than the profits of AMPP. On 15 October he was married to Alicia Knatchbull-Hugessen, youngest child of the first Lord Brabourne, who had married a second time in 1890, at the age of sixty, and had died in 1893, a fortnight before Alicia was born. She was to be a uniquely loyal and devoted wife, in the true meaning of those hackneyed words. Her natural enthusiasms were for poetry and pictures, and she later recalled that her career as a collector had begun at the age of nine with a collection of rabbits' front teeth. But these interests, which were, at any rate to begin with, more or less alien to Clive, were balanced by an automatic willingness to accept the fact that he did not share them, and a determination to be consistently loyal and helpful to him in all his activities. After the war she would accompany him on various visits to Chile, where her chief memories were of malodorous nitrate works, and where the time must have hung heavy on her hands while he immersed himself with his usual thoroughness in the activities and problems of the large combine of electrical companies which were at that time the chief activity of Whitehall Electric. Later on, when all the companies in Central and South America had been disposed of, she would go with him on a variety of business trips and, later still, on somewhat uninspiring holiday cruises. And throughout she would, in spite of her shyness, uncomplainingly entertain a wide range of business people with whom she can often have had little in common. In return for the untiring support that she gave him, she developed considerable self-confidence as a result of the ever practical and effective example that he quietly set her. Apart from her loyalty, he also came to be indebted to her for the development of an aesthetic and historical interest in houses and their contents which he already possessed to some degree. Without her, or someone like her (and there were precious few like her in the circles in which his bachelor life had been spent) his life would have been immeasurably less interesting both to himself and to others, and indeed his career would probably have been largely restricted to a long string of business successes and conventional sporting pastimes.

They had first met as children, and again in Australia when they had both stayed with Clive's sister Lady Denman at Government House. Although they were so different in temperament, the close friendship of the two sisters-in-law was to remain of great importance to both of them for the rest of their lives. In London they lived across the street from each other, and Balcombe and Parham are only half an hour apart. Later on, in the middle 1930s, when Clive took up sailing and jointly with the Denmans acquired a holiday house at Thorpeness, Alicia would avoid the chilly sailing expeditions, but was quite content to occupy herself indoors or better still to indulge in gentle Suffolk sightseeing.

They were married in London at Christ Church, Down Street, and Clive's five-year-old nephew, the present Lord Cowdray, was a page, together with his twin sister Angela, both dressed in handsome Cossack suits, 'as a pretty tribute to our brave Russian Ally'. *The Lady* was able to report that 'it is so seldom that one hears of anything but quiet and hurried weddings in these anxious days that it is quite a relief to tell you of one that was cheerful and well attended, though only a few relatives and very intimate friends assembled afterwards at 19 Curzon Street, lent by the Dowager Lady Brabourne.' Instead of the usual wedding flowers, the church contained decorations for the harvest festival, 'flowers and beautiful fruit, much of which had been given by Mr Alfred de Rothschild', whose town house was a short distance away. After a honeymoon spent touring the New Forest, they settled for a time at 49 Charles Street, where their eldest child Veronica was born the following August. Clive's formidable mother was not displeased with the match, though for some reason she took exception to the name Alicia, and insisted on addressing her daughter-in-law by her last name, Dorothea. Even this failed to ruffle Alicia, and she seems to have regarded it as just another aspect of married life which it was her duty to accept. It is a little difficult to imagine a bride of today, however genuinely loyal and devoted, accepting such treatment apparently without resentment, and even affectionately signing letters to her mother-in-law with the name that had been foisted on her.

In the course of the following year they acquired 32 Grosvenor Square, which was to remain their London home, with interruptions in the war of 1939, until it was re-acquired by the Grosvenor Estate in 1948, and later pulled down, along with its neighbours on the west side of the square, to make room for the new American Embassy. Until the acquisition of Parham, the Pearsons occupied Balcombe House, on the Denmans' estate, as a country retreat.

Clive was appointed to the main board of S. Pearson & Son on 1 November 1917. When the war was over, in February 1919, after the birth of his second daughter, Lavinia, he received a letter from his mother asking 'Do you want to go on *working* or is it Father's idea? Remember there is no halfway house.' It was perhaps a superfluous reminder. For the next thirty years Clive went on as he had begun, and his thoroughness and attention to detail are well illustrated by personal working notebooks. His portrait was painted by Herbert Olivier for the office, along with other directors, and on 3 June 1920 it was handed over to Lord Cowdray at a ceremony at the Cannon Street Hotel, which included a concert with humorous songs and recitations, performed by the Mex Musical Society. The most reassuring aspect of the evening for a confirmed music-hater like Clive must have been the words NO ENCORES printed firmly at the top of the programme. In the same year Clive and his father between them made a contribution of £50,000 to the new Chemical School at Cambridge, with similar donations coming from Burmah Oil and the Anglo-Persian Company. A third daughter, Dione, was born on 16 July.

In the following year there was another presentation, this time to Clive of a bust of his father by Hamo Thorneycroft. Clive evidently took a lot of trouble with his speech on this occasion, and his detailed notes for it have survived. He said of his father 'His motto is "Do it with thy might". I believe he privately adds "No eyewash and know your job".' (The quotation, from the Book of Ecclesiastes, in fact runs 'Whatsoever thy hand findeth to do, do it with thy might; for there is no work, nor device, nor knowledge, nor wisdom, in the grave, whither thou goest.') Clive went on to recall his days in the Mexican oilfield, at Potrero No. 4: 'an army of men on a reservoir, Mr Body's pipeline gang laying a kilometre of pipeline a day. Ten weeks of it, seven days a week, and at most times sixteen hours a day . . . I speak not as one lucky enough to have been born his son – and he has often told me that my luck lay rather in being the son of Lady Cowdray – but I speak in that to all of us he is the Chief.' He added that at first he was strongly disinclined to have anything to do with oil, 'but subtly I was initiated into its problems and thrills.'

3
Parham and Castle Fraser

When the Pearsons set about looking for a country house after the war was over, there had been an agricultural depression lasting several decades, with rental income on landed estates falling and the need to repair and modernise cottages and estate buildings constantly increasing. Unless there was income from town property or commercial activities of some kind to subsidise an agricultural estate, landowners had not been comfortably placed for many years, although since wages were low, large numbers of indoor and outdoor staff were employed who would otherwise have been jobless.

Lady Zouche, a peeress in her own right, had, with her husband Sir Frederick Frankland, inherited the Parham estate from a distant relation as recently as 1917. She was hardly in a position to maintain the estate, let alone to pay for the improvements and modernisation that were needed. Lord Cowdray, on the other hand, noted in 1921 that the assets of Pearson's in 1921 must be worth £10m, and he was reckoned the sixth richest man in England when he died in 1927. However dubious such statistics may be, the last years of his life were certainly marked by public generosity on a truly heroic scale. Apart from their public benefactions, which included a donation of £106,000 to the Cowdray Hospital Association in 1921, the Cowdrays were willing to set up Clive and his young family in considerable style. As has been seen, the keynote in Lady Cowdray's taste in everything from bicycles to bookplates lay in the direction of formal splendour, and she might well have considered the historical restoration of an old house the source of much unnecessary trouble. There is evidence that all her children sometimes felt that they were not living up to the style which she regarded as being in keeping with her husband's spectacular achievements, and the place that had been carved out for them in the world. Fortunately, however, the younger ones had also inherited an independence of character which gave them the confidence to follow standards and interests of their own choosing rather than of hers. Clive and Alicia, after toying with the idea of one or two

Clive, early 1890s.

Geoffrey, governess Xenia Maud Cooke, and Clive, c. 1894.

Clive's mother at Paddockhurst with a silver bicycle from Tiffany, c.1895.

Alicia with her mother, Lady Brabourne, and Prudence Sergison, c. 1903.

Clive's father: portrait by John Singer Sargent, at Cowdray.

Clive's sister, Trudie (Lady Denman), with Veronica.

Alicia, from a drawing by Percival Anderson, 1918.

From Vogue, March 1927: 'Veronica, Lavinia, Dione are the names of these charming people waiting to mount. They are the Hon. Clive Pearson's children, Lord Cowdray's grandchildren.'

Cowdray: line drawing by Lavinia.

other houses of a similar date, were immediately attracted by Parham, both for its own sake and for general convenience for London and for the homes of other members of the family, not least his sister Lady Denman at Balcombe. But Clive's approach to buying it was characteristically business-like and unhurried.

The Parham estate had amounted to over 6,000 acres in 1880, but piecemeal sales had reduced it to 3,700 acres by 1921. It approaches the village of Storrington at its eastern end, extends almost to Pulborough to the north, and to the west runs up to a point on the downs towards Arundel, which is marked by a boundary stone of great age, carved with the letter 'N', for Norfolk, on one side, and 'Z', for Zouche, on the other. The house is approached through an undulating park, which looks up to the steep line of the downs to the south and merges with the Sussex weald to the north. It is scattered with groups of venerable oak trees, many of them now sadly past their prime, and further damaged by two recent gales. They are interspersed with denser clumps of trees and with large beds of bracken, in which a herd of unusually dark fallow deer can escape from the heat and flies of summer, while in winter storms they have been known to wander onto a small lawn in the estate yard for shelter. As a result of the deer and their habits, the park has a natural, slightly shaggy air, in pleasing contrast to the results of modern farming methods elsewhere. The drive leads up to the north-east corner of the house, which from that angle does not give a striking first impression. Rather, it is a collection of buildings going back to the sixteenth century, with discreet and harmonious later alterations and additions, with the main front door now at the western end of the north front. It is reached through a courtyard flanked on its northern side by a pleasing stable block, now sympathetically adapted for other uses, pierced by an archway and crowned with a handsome clock-tower.

It is the south front, facing up to the ridge of the downs about a mile away, which is the great external feature of Parham. It is built of a rough, chalky local stone, known as 'clunch', with coigns and window surrounds of dressed stone, probably imported from Caen in Normandy, as for the cathedrals at Winchester and elsewhere in earlier centuries, and brought up the River Arun in barges. In 1920 the general taste of those who were not looking for a brand new house and were interested in the past was for the period before 1600. (The eighteenth century had remarkably few admirers until the 1930s, when the Georgian Group was founded by Lord Rosse and other enthusiasts who were appalled by the way in which classical architecture was disappearing, through indifference and neglect, all over England.) The heavy increase in taxation, and particularly in death duties, brought about by the 1914 war had come on top of financial difficulties for landowners already mentioned. Some great houses of the period, like Knole, Montacute and Blickling, were to pass into the hands of the National Trust, which was however at that time more concerned with acquiring open spaces in the countryside than with large houses in need of very expensive salvation. Moreover, the modern development of finding ingenious new uses for large houses had hardly begun. Occasionally a school or other institution moved in, but more often it was the demolishers' men. Parham was exceptionally lucky to attract new owners who could afford to bring it back to life with the Pearsons' rare mixture of energy, patience, ingenuity and tact.

The house at that time was without mains water, electricity or drains, and much of the extensive roof leaked badly. But Clive had been developing for the previous ten years the talent for organisation and above all exact costing that he had inherited from his father, and quickly worked out that £21,250 needed spending at once on the water and electricity supply and drives and estate roads. A careful comparison was also made of the cost of upkeep with the income and expenditure on the Cowdray estates. At Parham there were fewer cottages, which were regarded as a heavy liability, and lower costs on roads, fences and drainage. The conclusion was that Parham was easier to run, and there would be greater comforts. The original asking price in April 1920 was £200,000, and the reaction of Major Harding-Newman, the agent at Cowdray Park whose advice was gladly sought by Clive, was that the owners 'were asking enough, unless there's gold or oil there'. Clive, who had lived with his young family at weekends at a house on his sister Lady Denman's estate at Balcombe, less than an hour's drive from Parham, told Harding-Newman on 26 May 'I do not think we have entirely written off the estate as a possibility.' But Sir Frederick, who had complete charge of his wife's property, at first showed no signs of being willing to lower his price, and by March 1921 Clive again wrote to Harding-Newman, this time that 'we are not intending to pursue matters further, partly because the price is a stiff one, and partly because the place, with all that must be done with it, is somewhat larger than what we want', but adding that 'if you happen to hear that the price has become more reasonable you might please drop me a line'. By the middle of October Harding-Newman reported back that 'they seem to have made up their minds to clear out, as

Lady Zouche has mentioned one or two places with a view to taking or buying. I have got the impression that they really mean to sell.' The fact that in November of the previous year Lady Zouche had sold twenty-six lots of furniture from Parham is further evidence that something was in the air. In November Harding-Newman wrote that he was 'pleased to confirm that I have arranged with Frankland to buy Parham for you for £125,000, with an option to take over pictures and furniture not required by Sir Frederick and Lady Zouche at valuation, subject to the water supply being equal to your requirements'; and on 9 December 1921, 'We have finally purchased.' Harding-Newman had in fact been acting informally for Sir Frederick to find a buyer, and found himself, to his slight embarrassment, advising both sides on the deal. The question of his commission was therefore somewhat obscure, but was eventually settled rather generously by Clive paying him a fee of £1,466.

It has already been explained that Clive was in the process of taking over from his father the direction of much of the Pearson commercial empire, with the exception of the Westminster Press, which had been built up to control, among other things, sixteen provincial newspapers, and of which his brother Harold, soon to succeed briefly as second Lord Cowdray, became chairman. The time that he could devote to Parham was severely limited, and was further disrupted by long absences abroad on business, as will be seen later.

Being a trained engineer, Clive never undertook any project in a hurry or without looking at it from every angle. Later, when alterations to the house got under way, fresh discoveries were often made about the original structure during Clive's absences in North or South America. Before any decision was taken about how to proceed, there would be long and thorough exchanges of cables. As he was to do later at Castle Fraser, Clive took the utmost care not to introduce a jarring note in any modernisations or replacements that became necessary. On one occasion, when a rambling stretch of wall in the park at Parham had to be replaced, he took great exception to the new version, and made the estate workmen peg it out again with the old undulations. He liked work to be carried out by his own men, under his own absolute control.

On the first Sunday of the month there was an early Holy Communion service in the little church near the house at Parham, and the vicar would invariably have breakfast with Clive and Alicia afterwards and bring them up to date with matters of concern in the parish, until it was time for the second morning service at eleven. This was an excellent way of discovering information which might otherwise have come to his ears in a distorted form, if at all. There was a further invariable Sunday meeting with the head gardener at noon. But the Pearsons' interest in gardening was perfunctory: all that was required was a June border, and a subsequent Goodwood border, to look its best in the last week in July, for the high point of the local racing and polo seasons. As early as March 1922 Clive and Harold, as joint masters, had formed a pack of foxhounds called the Cowdray Hunt, kennelled at Cowdray, to hunt over the Goodwood country, previously hunted by Lord Leconfield, who had decided after the war to reduce his activities. This arrangement was warmly received in the local press, and was to work well for many years. One of the few hitches occurred when the staunchly Tory Lord Leconfield lent a particularly expert groom to help with the enlarged stables at Cowdray, where the hounds were kennelled. He later discovered that the Liberal Pearsons were making use of his groom to distribute what he regarded as pernicious political literature in the constituency. It was many years before relations between Petworth and Cowdray were repaired.

Relations with other neighbours were always better. In spite of being preoccupied with business and with endless projects at Parham, Clive took his local duties seriously, contributed to innumerable local societies and causes, and helped them in any way within his considerable power. He was thus seen to be a local benefactor, in the family tradition, and was rewarded by kind offers from the long-established pillars of West Sussex, as when the Duke of Richmond wrote to him in July 1923, to ask 'Have you any ladies staying with you for Goodwood who take a special interest in racing? If so I will be glad to send you tickets for them, if you will let me have their names, for the new Ladies' Gallery.'

Parham's historical character stimulated its new owners to preserve it and to make a series of alterations and reinstatements in a wonderfully faithful fashion, as well as acquiring, with the help of painstaking advisers, pictures and furniture which were either directly connected with the house (in the case of portraits), or were of the appropriate date. It is therefore worth at this stage going briefly over its history.

Parham derives its name from Pearham, the pear enclosure. The earliest documents relating to it indicate that it was bought by St Dunstan about 950 and presented to the Abbot of Westminster. In 1356 it is described as consisting of a thatched hall with a chamber, a kitchen (which survives to this day in what is probably something like its original form), and a grange for storing produce. It would have been occupied, together with the 600 acres of the manor, by a tenant of the Abbot. When the abbeys were dissolved, Parham would remain in the ownership of four generations of the Palmer family: Robert, a Sussex man well established in the cloth trade in London, who died in 1544; his son, Thomas, knighted by 1544; his grandson William, who married the heiress of Hugh Verney of Fairfield, near Bridgwater in Somerset, and whose descendants live there to this day. William's son, another Thomas, laid the first stone of the present house at Parham, at the age of two and a half, on 28 January 1577, following a custom of the time that it brought luck to have a foundation stone laid by a child. Nevertheless, he proved to be the last Palmer of Parham. Having served under Drake and Hawkins, he was knighted by the Lord High Admiral on his ship off Cadiz in 1596. But he then quarrelled with his wife, let Parham to Thomas Bysshopp, and sold it to him five years later. He then moved rather surprisingly to Spain, and settled down among his former enemies, dying there in 1605, still aged only thirty-five.

The new owner of Parham already possessed property in Sussex, at Henfield, was a member of the Inner Temple, and had sat in Parliament since 1584. He served as Secretary to Sir Francis Walsingham, was knighted by James I at Theobalds in 1605, and for a consideration of £1,600 was made a baronet in 1620. Parham would be inherited more than once through the female line, but Sir Thomas Bysshopp's descendants remained there, 'worthily if without much distinction' as Christopher Hussey put it in an article in *Country Life*, for 320 years from the date of his purchase of the property.

This is perhaps also the place to mention very briefly the main alterations that were made to the house between its first construction and its acquisition by the Pearsons, since as well as preserving what was best, another part of their work there was to lie in undoing or correcting what intervening generations had regarded as improvements, but which later appeared to be the opposite. In about 1710 a handsome doorway was added in the centre of the south front, at what was the main entrance to the house until the alterations that were made between 1830 and 1840. The stable block opposite the north front was built in 1778–9, when the last remains of the little medieval village which huddled round the church, facing the south front, were swept away. About the same time the delightful saloon on the west front was redecorated, and a marble fireplace installed, containing a plaque of Apollo and the Muses. Many of the present contents of that room were acquired and placed there to harmonise with the few existing contents of that date, such as the great Worcester dessert service commemorating the marriage of Cecil, son of the twelfth Lord Zouche, to Lady Charlotte Townshend, and displaying both their coats of arms. The Pearsons added in due course the delicate Sheraton beechwood chairs; the pair of views of the Thames in London by William James, and the most attractive group of portraits of John Fawcett and his wife and three young sons. The Green Room, directly above the saloon, now contains the collection centred round Sir Joseph Banks, the explorer and botanist who had sailed with Captain Cook to Australia, and whose wife was the sister of Alicia Pearson's great-grandmother. These important additions to the contents of Parham do much to fill the gap which would have been caused by the lack of any particularly remarkable or interesting members of the Bysshopp family in the seventeenth and eighteenth centuries, and they underline the fact that it was Alicia, just as much as Clive, who was to fill the house with beautiful and interesting contents.

Apart from Toby Fitzwilliam, Clive in his early life can hardly have come across, let alone made friends with, anyone interested in historic buildings or architecture, except for the purposes of self-aggrandisement. But fortunately for himself, and for Parham, he had married a wife with taste and powers of discernment which he recognised, enlisted and came to share. For some years after the acquisition of Parham, they bought pictures (including a further twenty-two from Lady Zouche) that were in some way connected with the royal and family portraits that were there already. Trouble was also taken to provide them with contemporary frames of high quality. And when they came to open Parham to the public, they were provided with a good reason to add further to what was already a greatly enhanced collection.

Between 1830 and 1840 the present entrance porch on the north front was added, together with the staircase inside it which leads up to the level of the Great Hall and the other south-facing rooms. Earlier, in the eighteenth century, the gables on the east and south fronts were built up into segmental profile, the ones on the south front having previously been altered into rounded forms. The mullioned windows were also replaced with sashes. It can thus be seen that the house never remained in a static condition for very long, and when the Pearsons, after the most thorough deliberations in the intervals of their absences abroad, came to make their own alterations both at Parham and Castle Fraser, it was almost always to restore the house in the spirit of its original design. They were not excessively puristic in their approach, and when there were good reasons to leave eighteenth-century innovations alone, as in the rooms in the west front already described, they were happy to do so. They were emphatically making a home, not a museum or a pedantic reconstruction. Their largest scale operations were to undo the work of a later generation of Bysshopps, who had removed the ceiling of the Great Parlour to make it the same height as the Great Hall next door. In 1924 this ceiling was replaced (seventeen inches higher than it had been originally) to give slightly more height to what was now a significant ground floor room. But the chief object was to provide Alicia with what was to become a delightful bedroom at the south-west corner of the first floor. The Knatchbull and Hugessen crests were installed for her above the south window, and a fine leopard, one of the Brabourne supporters, over the westerly window. A large and elaborate plaster overmantel was also added, featuring a view of the house, Clive's and Alicia's initials, and a selection of heraldic devices and other decorative motifs. They also lowered the ceiling in the dining-room at the south-east corner of the house, formerly a high and rather forbidding room which had also been remodelled in Victorian times, and filled it with pale and pleasing period panelling. Later, in 1933, after the arrival of numerous books from Paddockhurst, they created the South Library between the dining-room and the Great Hall. This was the room which in theory was their main sitting-room, and it remains to this day a private room, not shown to the public.

All through the 1920s and 1930s there was always work going on, and generally some scaffolding about on the outside walls, where new windows were needed to light the altered rooms. The family were always ready to migrate from room to room as work progressed. But at first, Clive's approach is summed up by a letter he wrote to a common friend when a dealer in Duke Street had solicited some work: 'I did not tell him we hope to rub along with some white-washing and not to give the place over to decorators!' The new library was embellished when Clive acquired, as usual on the recommendation of the indispensable Victor Heal, the panelling of an entire seventeenth-century house in Soho Square, which contained two carved fireplaces and overmantels. This was chiefly installed at 32 Grosvenor Square, but only one of the fireplaces was needed there and the other was installed in the new library at Parham, together with other appropriate panelling. But so that it could afterwards be seen what had been done, Clive was careful to put the panelling on hinges, and the original state of the room can still therefore be traced.

This library-sitting-room was not where Clive worked when he was at home. He set up a working library at the west end of the house, and gradually collected a group of reference works which within its limits is comprehensive as regards the study of architecture and the arts and their history, as well as containing everything that might be needed concerning local history in Sussex. This room has been occupied since his death by those who are responsible for the arrangements for opening the house, and it provides the answer to any question that can reasonably be asked concerning the house and its history, and a great deal more besides. Two years later, in 1935, he commissioned Esmond Burton, who was already responsible for the plasterwork in Alicia's bedroom, to create a fine plasterwork ceiling in the Great Hall and in the Great Parlour next door, where a frieze was created, featuring crests and charges from the coats of arms of the various families connected with Parham's history: Bysshopp, Knatchbull impaling Dering, Southwell impaling Dering, and finally Pearson impaling Knatchbull-Hugessen.

The summer of 1921 had been particularly dry, and as soon as the purchase of Parham was completed, Harding-Newman reported to Clive that the springs from which the house was supplied with water had run dry for the first time for forty years. Both the water and electricity supplies were quite insufficient for a modern household run on the lines which Clive required, and his own lengthy pencilled calculations on the number of gallons of water needed daily by up to forty people were as exact as if they had been made in the oilfields of Mexico. Electricity needs for lighting the house (for the first time), for the fire pump, the laundry and the farm could easily be calculated by the man who was shortly to arrange for the street lighting of Santiago. In 1924 estimates were obtained for the cost of installing windmills, one for pumping water and doing other farm work, and the other for providing power for the three hundred lights in the house itself. In 1932 *The Times* printed a very long letter, complete with map, from Professor C. E. M. Joad, the popular philosopher later better known for his contributions to the Brains Trust (and later still for fare-dodging on the railway) protesting eloquently against the threat of a line of electricity pylons which would ruin the appearance of Amberley village and the famous Wild Brooks nearby, at the western end of the Parham estate. As part of his general sense of local responsibility, Clive kept a watchful eye on any development that could affect the area, and at one crucial stage he characteristically summoned the Clerk of the West Sussex County Council to breakfast at Parham 'at 8 a.m. or thereabouts' before a meeting in the park with members of the Chanctonbury Rural District Council. Other memoranda from him survive on all manner of points of detail down to the cost of draining-boards for decanters in the pantry. A steam tractor had cost as much as £960 in 1918. The horse that pulled the mowing-machine was called Lord Zouche, and when he eventually retired, the cost of a small motor-mower was £75.

A good example of Clive's attention to detail, and the trouble he took about delegating responsibility effectively, was his firm rule never to employ an estate agent who was unable or unwilling to go about his work on horseback. Otherwise there would always be inaccessible corners of the estate which involved too much time or trouble to reach, and would inevitably be neglected. This attitude no doubt had its origins in Clive's university training in the mechanical sciences, and his visits to Mexico soon afterwards. Few landowners of his time can have looked after their property with such meticulous care, and few were in a position to pay such attention to living conditions, or could afford to instal modern sanitation and comforts in innumerable old cottages. But just as his father had done in the swamps of Mexico, so at Parham Clive took the view that if you want good people to work for you, you must look after them properly. All this earned him respect, sometimes tinged with fear: he could be crushing, but he was never ultimately unfair, and his underlying generosity when he felt it was deserved meant that he often kept on farm workers beyond retiring age so that, if they wished, they would not be entirely dependent on their pensions. Altogether, he ran Parham, as he ran Pearson's, on business lines, benevolently but firmly, and keeping to a clear management structure. Casual acquaintances often found him gruff and even formidable, partly as a result of his shyness, but also because he was by training strict, and impatient with any signs of incompetence, slovenliness or failure to carry out instructions. An eminently practical approach had already become second nature to him, and partly out of natural reserve, but more out of long-established business habits, he did not go in for any easy camaraderie with people who worked for him, and his approach was not that of an old-fashioned landowner of long standing who would have known the families working on the estate for many years, but it was sensible and fair, and everyone knew where they stood.

On his Sunday tours of inspection he had an uncanny flair, in the words of one of his surviving farm managers, for 'putting his finger on the weak spot: if there was a corner of a farm which you would prefer him not to see, or where some unfortunate delay had occurred, he would invariably seek it out'. Rather surprisingly, before the days of Land Rovers, he would set off on these tours, accompanied by the relevant head of department, in an old Rolls-Royce, which was often to be seen in the middle of muddy fields and in other improbable places. Far from being a status symbol, a car was simply a vehicle to take him to his destination, and it just so happened that a Rolls-Royce was the best make, the most reliable and the most durable; so he used one. If he was a hard taskmaster, and a very careful calculator of costs, he was certainly neither mean nor grasping. One of his daughters remembers the case of a footman at Parham who was caught out in a minor theft. This was reported to Clive, and he was asked if he intended to prosecute, but his reply was no, the man's wages had better be increased. Two years before his death, when he went off on a winter cruise, his secretary at Parham, Rosemary Courcier, wrote to him: 'I feel deeply beholden to you for innumerable acts of kindness and generosity . . . for allowing me so much freedom to look after Mother when there was so much work to be done. I shall be hoping the trip to Cape Town will be the greatest success . . . we shall be missing you both all the time and longing to have you home again.' No harsh employer would have received such a letter, and the powerful loyalty that was felt by those who worked for him for any length of time is absolute proof of his human qualities.

He also did his best to solve problems for other members of the family. His mother's sister, 'Aunt Arab', who settled at Parham in 1940 for the duration of the war, was bemused by the problem of making her will, and which of her possessions to leave to whom, and consulted Clive. After listening patiently to her rambling predicament, he eventually told her that it was quite simple: she should leave everything to him, and in due course he would see that those concerned received fair shares, according to their needs and tastes. Indeed, this is what eventually happened, and the episode is typical of Clive at his conscientious, fair-minded, practical best.

Parham was not to be Clive's only major acquisition in 1921, but the Scottish property that he was given must have come as a distinct surprise. Lord Cowdray had bought Dunecht, a vast grey stone mansion fifteen miles west of Aberdeen, in 1909. It came with 9,000 acres, but he had then spent further large sums adding to the estate and building cottages, schools, clubs and playing fields, till in 1923 the property extended to nearly 28,000 acres. The neighbouring estate at Castle Fraser, of another 2,300 acres, had first come to his attention in 1916 when it became known that the owner, Mrs Frederick Mackenzie Fraser, a childless, Irish-born widow, was in a sadly impoverished state and might be obliged to sell. On 3 October Lord Cowdray wrote to his accountant in Edinburgh that following on a conversation between them he was afraid that she was 'buoying herself up in the belief that it was our wish to purchase', whereas it was Mrs Fraser 'who had suggested to us that she would like us to buy the property'; and 'we should only be prepared to buy on present commercial values'. He added that the estate 'would be a fine addition to Dunecht', but 'it would be far more convenient to purchase it say two years after the war when we know how things are. Rather than risk the property passing us by we should (corrected to 'might') be prepared to buy today.'

There were to be many ups and downs before the estate was acquired. In November 1919 that important pillar of Pearsons Mr C. Reed (as he was always referred to in full by Clive) wrote a memorandum in 47 Parliament Street saying 'Will you please note that in all probability some £45,000 will be needed by the Chief on February 2nd in connection with the purchase of Castle Fraser.' At this stage, all seemed settled. However, endless prevarication followed and nearly eighteen months later, on 7 June 1921, Cowdray wrote to his agents, Brodies, that 'we have definitely decided not to purchase it' and that Mrs Mackenzie Fraser was 'impossible'; the other reasons being that 'the number of small holdings on the estate and the bad condition of the property generally' would mean that it 'would give us more trouble than pleasure'. An auction had been announced for 9 August, and Cowdray added that 'we shall probably bid for some lots contiguous with Dunecht estate if Castle Fraser is not sold as a whole'. But on 21 June, by now quite fed up with the twists and turns of the vendor, or her lawyers, or both, he wrote again that 'we are not prepared to reopen negotiations nor to bid for the property if put up for auction'. Yet at the very last minute something made him change his mind again. Was this genuine, or part of an elaborate stratagem to retaliate against the tricky (or confused) owner? In all probability the former, for on 6 August he wrote to Brodies from Carlsbad: 'Notwithstanding my former decision not to buy I should be prepared to buy at a commercial price. Thus kindly keep your ears and eyes open'; and on the 9th, only ten days before the auction, he instructed Brodies to bid up to £50,000 or so, adding, interestingly, that 'Donside properties have no amenities or charms like Deeside . . . The castle itself is perfectly charming, and so are the immediate surroundings. But there is no shooting or fishing or society, and no money has been spent on its upkeep for 20 years. Unless we get it at a low figure, it cannot be a joy to us whatever it may be to our descendants.' He had, as usual, judged the costing to perfection. On the 19th, after the auction was over, Brodies wired 'Castle Fraser purchased for £48,000.' The *Aberdeen Free Press* of 21 August had announced the auction, adding that 'the building is of unique architectural and historical interest and it should be secured as a national monument. The Government itself cannot be expected to buy it, but some wealthy donor may see his way to acquire it for the nation'! In a roundabout way, this is in fact what ultimately happened via Lord Cowdray and the National Trust for Scotland.

It appears that Cowdray proceeded to offer it both to his elder son Harold, and also to Trudie, but that both quickly declined it, leaving Clive, who was already attracted to the castle and had in the past now and then bicycled over to Castle Fraser and established cordial relations with the owner, in possession. In October Brodies wrote to Cowdray inquiring whether 'in view of the fact that your Lordship is to make over the estate to the Hon. Clive Pearson' a separate system of accounts was to be set up for the estate, and received the answer that a new bank account was to be opened, and operated by the factor and Mr Clive. It was, incidentally, only six weeks later that Clive received the news that Parham was to be his as well. But the details of the transfer of Castle Fraser seem to have been left surprisingly vague, or perhaps with so much else to occupy his attention, Clive temporarily lost sight of them. But as late as March 1926 he wrote to Brodies that 'I cannot put my hand on any document to show whether or not Castle Fraser is my own property or whether I hold it under some settlement or other'. They replied that 'this estate is your own absolute property'. A year before, they had in fact informed him that it was his father's wish that while the estate should be conveyed to him outright, an obligation should be imposed that in the event of Clive or his successors selling it, it should first be offered to the proprietor of Dunecht, if a member of the Cowdray family. They added, rather surprisingly, that such a stipulation could not be legally effective; but 'the Disposition is docqueted to this effect so that if the occasion should arise the intention should not be lost sight of'. Among the various hitches that had arisen in the course of the sale was the removal of an elaborate sundial by Mrs Mackenzie Fraser and her subsequent discovery that there were a few objects in the castle (valued at £110.17s6d) which had been included in the sale but which she in fact wished to retain. She offered to return the sundial in exchange for them, but Clive's reaction was that she could have them for cash but not in exchange for something that was, or should have been, his already.

Obviously, Castle Fraser was only to be a holiday home for Clive and his family. He was working full time in London ('no half way house') and Parham was his weekend retreat, within convenient reach. As has been seen, he and Alicia set themselves plenty of work to do there as well, but it was work of such an infinitely congenial kind as to become a real relaxation from office life and travel abroad, even though it was carried out to the same meticulous standard. As things turned out, it was not until most of the reorganisation of Parham was completed that serious alterations were embarked on at Castle Fraser. As at Parham, there were many later structural alterations to be undone, and photographs show more vividly than any words could do the state of the High Hall under Mrs Mackenzie Fraser's occupation and the characteristically faithful and discreet way in which Clive restored it to something very like its original condition. What was that condition, and how had it come about?

In the middle of the fifteenth century King James II of Scotland was breaking up what had been a large, semi-independent area of the Earldom of Mar, and in 1454 granted the lands of Muchall and Stoneywood to Thomas Fraser in exchange for his property at Cornton in Stirlingshire. The origins of Castle Fraser probably lie in a substantial stone tower, built by him in a sheltered position (for Aberdeenshire) and surrounded by undulating farm land and woods. By the mid-1570s his successor Michael Fraser's branch of the family had steadily increased in significance as a result of marriages with the daughters of local lairds. Possibly to mark this upward trend, he embarked on a massive remodelling of the castle, adding two towers at the north-east and south-east corners. His son Andrew, who held the castle from 1588 till 1636, and was made Lord Fraser three years before his death, continued his father's work, extending the main tower westwards and adding two further floors to the whole building. He probably finished external works in 1618, since that is the date carved on the gable overlooking the present courtyard, above the massively carved royal coat of arms, with those of Fraser of Muchall below. Without going into the various problems and uncertainties which surround the question of when the various additions were made, it is enough to say that the lower storeys of the castle are plain and unadorned, but designed in satisfying proportions and built of local stone, partly harled in an attractive off-white colour; while the upper turrets and window-frames are richly decorated with a profusion of carving. The crest of the weather-cock on the turret overlooking the drum-shaped staircase-tower is ninety-one feet above the ground, and the overall impression which the castle gives is first one of height, but then one of harmonious solidarity as well.

King George V and Queen Mary and the present Queen Mother went over from Dunecht to inspect Castle Fraser in the absence of its owners in 1925. It is fairly clear that Lady Cowdray considered that Castle Fraser was in some respects inadequate for a man in Clive's position, and commended to him the services of the most fashionable Scottish architect of the day, Sir Robert Lorimer. All that Clive wanted from him was a set of historical drawings, so that nineteenth-century disfigurements of the castle, and other earlier alterations, could be undone. What Sir Robert wanted was something quite different, namely to provide accommodation for numerous shooting guests complete with their own attendants, as well as for all those who might be needed to look after the Pearson children. But although there was good rough shooting at Castle Fraser, Clive never seems to have had the time or the inclination to go out himself, let alone to invite large parties. He had plenty on his hands at Parham, in London and, indirectly, in many other parts of the world as well, and he tried to head off Sir Robert from the start, writing in his first letter to him 'I am not desirous to contemplate any actual alterations – anyhow until a later date.' After further exchanges, Lorimer produced plans in 1926. As John Cornforth has rightly pointed out in his two articles on Castle Fraser in *Country Life* in August 1978, 'to most people's eyes they would have wrecked the place'. They involved adding an extra storey above the two wings which flank the courtyard, demolishing the lodges in which the wings terminate, and building another wing to close off the courtyard, with a main entrance in the middle and a new staircase inside. Clive was well able to resist this grandiose plan, and in March 1927 wrote 'I have the impression that our scheming has been too drastic.' It seems likely that he had not found much time to consider what he really wanted, and it is not clear exactly what Lorimer had been asked to provide: no doubt Clive's request for ideas was made in very general terms, for he went on to say 'We ought perhaps to proceed on the basis of fitting ourselves into the Castle as she is, with the minimum of disturbance.' Sir Robert was not surprisingly 'rather disappointed', and plainly thought it would be quite unsuitable for the family to fit itself into the castle by themselves, with only three or four servants, and without the horde of visiting chauffeurs, loaders and ladies' maids that his other rich clients usually wanted. What he could not or would not understand was that the Pearsons only wanted to spend three or four weeks a year there with their family every summer. As it turned out, Lorimer died in 1929 before anything was done. The family would at first spend their holiday based on Dunecht, where there was no shortage of space, and Clive would at first take them over to Castle Fraser himself. His daughter Lavinia, to whom the property was handed over in 1946 after the return of her husband Major Michael Smiley from a prisoner of war camp in Germany, has given a delightful picture of the children's visits to the castle when they were old enough to drive over in a pony-cart from Dunecht by themselves. They would roam happily through the large walled garden amongst the scented stocks and phlox, the clumps of pampas grass and the broken pump, and feast on the raspberries and red currants.

In the last few years before 1939 Clive converted the hollow circle of the stables nearby, with its entrance arch flanked by shapely conical turrets, into an ideal holiday home, from which the castle itself could slowly be given back its original character. Lavinia recalled that to her father, the castle was a beautiful and romantic building, crying out to have its wrongs patiently and skilfully put right. To the children it was 'a broken down, spooky old place', where they could give each other delicious frights and revel in the housekeeper's stories of bloodstains on the stone stairs which could never be washed out. On a sunny summer's day nowhere could have a pleasanter and more cheerfully bracing atmosphere than the castle and its surroundings. But the sun does not always shine in Scotland, and on darker days Lavinia heard phantom workmen hammering, a distant baby crying, and even the clash of swords.

After the death of Lorimer, Clive found a much more congenial collaborator in the shape of Dr William Kelly, a recently retired architect from Aberdeen whose chief interest fortunately lay in scholarly research and restoration. By September 1937 a thorough archaeological survey under his direction was under way. Blocked up windows were then reopened, masonry and plaster were stripped from the Great Hall, and lath and more plaster removed from the walls of the Square Tower. Dr Kelly worked on in November, and reported to Alicia in his unique handwriting which recalls an Elizabethan charter that 'My wife and I spent a delightful week there; it did not feel at all cold in the castle; I suppose the thick walls (like the sea) retain their summer heat for some time.' More work of a similar kind was carried out after the family's summer visit in 1938. It went on through the winter, and Clive was lucky in having a factor, Alan Marshall, who fully shared his antiquarian interests and was capable of submitting carefully thought out proposals, including details of types of door, casement or sash windows, heads and spouts for drainpipes, and the exact amount of space to be left under the floorboards. When Lorimer was still on the scene, Marshall had commented in one of his regular letters to Clive that 'you will note that Sir Robert suggests a bell shaped turret roof instead of the present straight pitch. I do not know how far he is right in this respect; he says it is "very Aberdeen", although I must say I do not recollect seeing any of this type in Aberdeenshire.' Without someone of Marshall's calibre, the alterations and improvements could never have been carried out to Clive's satisfaction, and even so problems arose as a result of Clive's control being so remote. In January 1939 he complained that 'it sadly seems that our importing skilled townsmen to do the work has led to a modern finish which might have been more easily avoided if we had been employing our own people . . . I expect it is a matter of using a different type of tool; if perchance they have been using a steel trowel they will I expect have to change to an instrument of wood.'

By the end of July, other preoccupations were in the air. Preparations for the war varied in different parts of the country. In the south-east of England, where air raids and even invasion threatened, all kinds of plans went ahead for evacuating civilians, equipping them with gas-masks and ration books, digging air-raid shelters and even putting up obstacles against tanks. In the north-east of Scotland a calmer atmosphere prevailed, and at the end of July substantial emergency stores were laid in, rather as if the Mackenzie Frasers were expecting trouble from a neighbouring clan. On 27 July 2 cwt of granulated and ½ cwt of Demerara sugar were prudently acquired, together with 60 2 lb tins of syrup and 24 of treacle, 28 lb of lentils, 14 lb of barley, and a hundredweight of pale soap.

On the outbreak of war in 1939, eight of the estate staff joined the forces at once, and refugee families appeared from Clydeside, only to disappear again out of dislike of the remote Aberdeenshire countryside and preference for home surroundings whatever the dangers and shortages might be. To help feed the schoolchildren who were installed at

Parham, a good supply of vegetables was sent down from Castle Fraser in December, and more were asked for. 4 cwt of beetroots and one of carrots were followed by 300 lambs for fattening, and raspberries and the cones of *Abies nobilis* also made their way south. (Parham, having by then a huge population to feed, was only able to reciprocate with six damson trees.) Brigade HQ for 153 Brigade, Highland Division, was set up in the castle in 1941, without mishap. Building work had continued slowly in spite of the war, and was only halted when the indispensable Dr Kelly had the misfortune to break his leg in 1941 and was obliged to give up his direction of the scheme. This is not the place to quote his historical research at length, but he was the ideal man to advise Clive, and their collaboration was a happy one on both sides.

From the earliest stages, Clive's two estates helped each other reciprocally. In the winter of 1926–7, 2,000 sycamore seedlings and 700 ash were sent down from Castle Fraser to Parham, in return for 2,000 beech plants from Parham. The agent there, Sherston, at one time wrote to Marshall ruefully that he had 'lately purchased what is commonly known in England as a Scotch cart, i.e. a low, two-wheeled, flat-bottomed cart, without sides. Mr Pearson tells me it is a very poor imitation of the proper thing, and he would very much like you to send me a cutting out of a catalogue, in order that I may know what a Scotch cart really is!' The next year Marshall wrote to Clive 'You will be pleased to hear that I have this year again beaten Dunecht with the price of lambs, 39 shillings against 34'. Later, Clive undertook to spend £46 on the rebuilding of the organ in the church at Kemnay, but not a further similar sum on installing an electric blower.

After the war Clive handed over Castle Fraser to his daughter Lavinia, at a time when her husband, after five years in a prisoner of war camp, wanted to farm but was unable to find a suitable property to buy in the neighbourhood of Parham, where they would have preferred to settle. Clive continued to help with Castle Fraser in all sorts of ways, and an example of the trouble he would take to make sure that everything was done right is in a typical letter he wrote on the retirement of the old factor: 'Whatever pension you may arrange, it would no doubt be much appreciated if you also paid him a lump sum to help with his removal expenses . . . and arrange the description and the time of payment so that it may be received free of tax and yet be chargeable against the estate as a maintenance claim.' On another occasion, he commented on a letter written by Lavinia when she was giving up an Edinburgh accountant of long standing in favour of one much nearer to hand in Aberdeen: 'Just now and again, on occasions which are surprisingly rare, there appears the perfect letter; perfect in clarity, and the decisiveness of its terms, its balanced expression and its courtesy. Such is yours to Jim Mounsey.' It is not difficult to see the source from which these qualities were inherited.

4
Chile

In order to see Clive's business activities in the 1920s in clear focus, it is necessary to look briefly at what had been going on in S. Pearson & Son since the major discoveries of oil in the triumphant years of 1910–11. The first consequence had been Lord Cowdray's decision to scale down the contracting work undertaken by the company, though exceptions were made in the case of the harbour works at Valparaiso, which began in 1912 and were not finally completed until 1924, and the post-war construction of the Sennar Dam in the Sudan. But chief priority was to be given to drilling for oil, and to the ancillary services required for refining, transporting and marketing it.

To this end Cowdray had from 1905 onwards successfully established the Puebla Tramway Light and Power Company, to which two more hydro-electric developments in Mexico and a second power plant were soon added. This experience was to show the way ahead when similar work was undertaken in Chile after the war, in the hinterland of the Valparaiso docks. But an even stronger reason for concentrating on the creation of public utilities elsewhere was the fact that from the fall of Cowdray's friend and ally President Diaz in 1911, Mexico remained in a fluctuating state of revolution until 1917. Even in the intervals of calm, no government had much control over the country and life and property were constantly at risk. There were vast amounts of oil in the ground and by the dedication of the staff of Mexican Eagle, under very difficult and often dangerous conditions, the company continued to prosper and supplied over 200,000 tons of oil a year to the Admiralty. But with endless political uncertainties surrounding the whole question of foreign interests in Mexico, Cowdray decided it would be wise to sell control of the company to a buyer in whom he could feel real confidence, who would be strong enough to hold it together in unpredictable circumstances and could give it undivided attention. (It should not be forgotten that besides his vast business responsibilities, Cowdray had served as the first President of the Air Board throughout 1917, and only resigned under insulting and quite undeserved provocation from Northcliffe and Lloyd George.)

Some idea of the growth of Mexican Eagle may be gained by considering that the company's capital had increased from 30 million Mexican dollars in 1908 to 86 million in 1920. But by the end of the war the company was isolated between Standard Oil of New Jersey and Royal Dutch Shell. And as that great analyst of the world struggle for oil, Dr Pierre L'Espagnol de la Tramerie, wrote in 1921, 'Isolated producers sometimes lack markets, especially if they are far removed from great centres of consumption.' Standard Oil tried to buy out Pearson's in 1911, and Royal Dutch followed in 1913, offering Pearson £2.15s a share when he asked for £3. By Tramerie's calculations, the lowest price of the shares in 1912 was 36 francs; in 1918, 83 francs; in 1919, 126; and in 1918 no less than 398 francs. Thus in eight years the value of the company had increased tenfold. When Royal Dutch finally returned to the attack in 1920, its chairman, Sir Henri Deterding, offered Cowdray £6 a share, and he accepted. There was enough oil in the territories owned by Mexican Eagle to triple the output, even from its new record level. But even Cowdray was not inclined to find the huge further sums needed to produce it. And the acquisition by Royal Dutch meant that Shell could ensure a supply of oil for the Royal Navy for the foreseeable future. Patriotically as well as commercially, Lord Cowdray could feel well satisfied.

As soon as it became known that Mexican Eagle was heading for success, other powerful interests made efforts to gain a share in the potential profits. Standard Oil itself had made further overtures in 1913, but since the company was already supplying oil to the Admiralty, Cowdray gave an undertaking to Lloyd George, who was then Chancellor of the Exchequer, not to sell the company, and to remain responsible for the Admiralty's supply, provided the Government would invest £5m in the company. Lloyd George refused, and when Standard Oil made a further offer in 1916, Cowdray was actually threatened with the Defence of the Realm Act unless he broke off negotiations. Thus the same government that created him a viscount in 1917 in effect not only refused him the national support that he needed and fully deserved, but also prevented him from seeking it elsewhere. Even by Lloyd George's standards, this was an amazing response to patriotism and loyalty. But Cowdray's endurance was finally rewarded in October 1918, when the Royal Dutch group spontaneously approached him. They were exactly the partners he needed. Early in 1919 they took over the management control, leaving the Cowdray interests as the next biggest shareholders until 1938, as will be shown later. Under Royal Dutch, Mexican Eagle's oil production rose from 18.7 million barrels in 1919 to 32 million in 1922. In that year, however, seepage of salt water into the wells caused grave problems, and Cowdray, who was by then aged sixty-six, must have been content that for once it was for others to solve them.

Following the experience that had been so successfully gained in the electrical enterprises in Mexico at Tampico, Vera Cruz, Orizaba and Cordoba, an obvious course was to look out for similar opportunities in other industrially backward countries. Since the company was heavily involved in the harbour works at Valparaiso, there was plainly scope for the development of electricity on the same sort of basis as at the Mexican ports. It so happened that the existing Chilean Electric Tramway and Light Company had been owned by a German company, which had placed the certificates on deposit with a German bank in London, where the company had become forfeit to the British Government. It had been run since 1914 by a London firm of engineers called J. G. White, which put in a bid when the shares were put up for sale by sealed tender by the Public Trustee. However, Pearson's bid was appreciably higher and was accepted. The first need was to eradicate German associations without damaging business relations in what was then (and was to remain in some degree to the present day) a very small business world in which everyone knew everyone else. In May 1920 Clive wrote that the company was 'still in the difficult position of not paying adequate wages, which cannot be rectified until the tramway tariff is revised'. By September Cowdray had invested £1.25m in the business through his holding company Whitehall Securities, which had originally been formed in 1907 to own shares and securities either in lieu of payment for work carried out by S. Pearson & Son Ltd or to enable clients to give contracts, or even sometimes to help clients solve their own difficulties. The most significant example of all was the fact that the Tehuantepec Railway was owned jointly by the Mexican government and Pearson's. The proceeds of the sale of control of Mexican Eagle to Royal Dutch also in due course flowed into Whitehall Securities, which was consequently in a position to make important new investments in promising new fields. This, indeed, became Clive's most significant and time-consuming task between the wars. One of these, as has been seen, was the Whitehall Electric Co. Lord Cowdray's legendary skill at costing new projects was brought to bear on Chile, and he took characteristic trouble himself to compare the estimates for the acquisition of the two original electricity companies at Santiago and Valparaiso with the figures for operating similar companies in Mexico. But the chief snag about this investment which would not become apparent till later, was the underlying resentment, partly no doubt increased artificially for political reasons, against an English company providing and controlling such a crucial public service, even though the Chileans were manifestly incapable of organising it for themselves at the time.

After taking over the two existing Chilean electricity companies and forming the Compania Chilena de Electricidad, the next step was to build new hydro-electric plants at Maitenes in the Andes, and later on the Maipo river. This enormously increased the supply available, which had previously depended entirely on an inadequate system at La Florida Falls outside Santiago, which was itself also acquired in 1923.

As in Mexico, Cowdray realised the great desirability of the operating company in Chile being a national one, with at least something in the way of genuine national roots, rather than being run exclusively for the benefit of British capitalists. Indeed, to support this general aim, a report from the Foreign Office on the Valparaiso Tramway Company explained that it was in German (Chilean) hands, and if it was bought 'it is doubtful if a British buyer would be accepted, and recommended the formation of a company nominally Chilean, with a combination of British and Chilean capital.' This is what then happened, though under £1m of the original capital was owned by Chileans, even though subscribers were given the added attraction of substantial discounts on their light and power bills.

Raising the capital for this, as well as for the other projects started by Whitehall Electric, was facilitated by the fact that Clive had joined the board of Lazards in 1920, and the chairman, Lord Kindersley, had given him a room of his own at the bank, telling him that 'we will thus have the advantage of more frequent consultations with you upon many matters in which your experience would be valuable to us, and you I believe would be able to enlarge your experience of foreign banking.' Among the benefits to the bank which arose from Clive's participation were, first, Lazards' offer for sale of £1m 6% First Mortgage Debenture Stock in Whitehall Electric Investments (1925–49), and a further £2½m the following year. The bank also offered for sale £1m 7½% Cumulative Preference Shares of £1 each at par in 1921, and another £2½m the following year. Lazards later also handled other issues of stock in

Newcastle-on-Tyne Electric Supply Ltd, West of England Electric Investments, South Wales Electric Power, and Wessex Electricity Co. Clive remained a director of Lazards until 1938, but with one crucial exception which will be described in due course he does not appear to have played much part in the bank's affairs other than attending monthly board meetings and making the odd shrewd comment. He took no files relating to Lazards back with him to Parham when he retired, and no details of his participation have been preserved at the bank.

The Chilena had a concession to run the tramways for a period of thirty years ending in 1932, so that when Clive sold out the Chilean interests of Pearson's in 1928 it had only four years to run. The trams had always been unprofitable to Pearson's, since the level of fares demanded was a very hotly disputed point, with many of the inhabitants of Santiago being too poor to be able to pay more than a token fare, so that the ticket rate became a political football, with each new set of politicians promising a still lower rate. The profits of the Chilena in 1922 were £161,661, and in 1923 £191,708, rising to £274,072 in 1927 and £348,787 in 1928. Their significance to Pearson's therefore overtook that of the corresponding company Mexican Electric & Power, which made contributions to Whitehall Securities of £244,250 in 1922–3, and £200,681, £96,427, £136,910 and £129,172 in the next four years.

By the time the Chilena was formed, Pearson's reputation was such that if Lord Cowdray decided to invest in a country he could attract the participation of the most prominent and influential national figures in banking, commerce and the law, as well as the pick of the engineering profession. Its first vice-president was Don Ismael Tocornal, who had headed a special trade mission to London in 1919, when Clive had given a large lunch party for him at 32 Grosvenor Square. In due course he became president of the Central Bank of Chile, and was replaced at the Chilena by Pedro Torres, who remained a faithful ally of Clive long after the sale of the Chilena. But perhaps most remarkable of Clive's Chilean colleagues was the engineer Don Juan Tonkin. Although his relations with Pearson's were to end on an unhappy note, his services to the Chilena were enormous. His English mother had earned great respect for her devoted collaboration with the wife of the British Minister, Mrs Kennedy, in an outbreak of cholera in 1888, and his father had been a notable engineer in the north of Chile, and had played an important part in civil works at the time of the War of the Pacific, when Chile defeated both Peru and Bolivia in the early 1880s. Juan Tonkin was born in 1875 and was thus thirteen years older than Clive. At the age of twenty-one, he had invented a machine for obtaining motive power from the waves of the sea, and as a young man he had worked for ten years on various projects in the USA including the Singer Building and the Hippodrome Theatre in New York, and the Baltimore-Ohio railway. He had then joined J. G. White and had been involved in the access works at the Pearson's undertaking at the Port of Valparaiso, and had had personal dealings with no less than seven Presidents of Chile. And it was he who had brought into being the Compania Nacional de Fuerza Electrica, which together with the Chilean Electric Tramway and Light Co. were the original elements of the Compania Chilena de Electricidad.

He then proceeded to take charge of a press campaign to bring public opinion round in favour of street lighting, declaring that its present state in Santiago 'would be shameful in any town in Africa'. His willingness to join forces with Pearson's arose from his feeling that 'it is better to be the tail of a lion than the head of a mouse'. Nevertheless he had to tread carefully, especially in his relations with various American companies which went back far beyond his involvement with Pearson's: the Americans were jealous of any extension of British interests in Chile, which they rightly saw as serious competition for their own plans. As a result of his efforts, the leading Chilean newspaper referred to 'the immense impulse being given to Chile's manufacturing industry when the hydro-electric schemes organised in 1921 are complete . . . S. Pearson & Son are famous for their brilliant water-harnessing and engineering works in many other regions.'

As early as 1922 Tonkin achieved his first great success for Pearson's when the general electricity tariff was doubled, with the approval of Congress. Lord Cowdray accepted that this was largely due to Tonkin's representations, and shrewdly recommended giving him 'some silver, gold-washed, table ornament, to cost between £300 and £500; presentation to be deferred till a suitable occasion such as the installation of a new power. Otherwise the opponents of the new tariff scale might harp on the magnificent bargain the company has made.' Tonkin was also at least partly responsible for the company's enlightened policy in establishing a large medical, sickness and benevolent fund for the employees, 'since the worker's only capital is usually his health'. A school, a shop, and an athletic club were also built at the new plant in Maitenes, rather in the same way as for the estate workers at Dunecht. When it was completed, at a cost of £950,000, the new plant made a total supply of 140,000 h.p.

available for public services, domestic utilities and the needs of industry. Clive had been determined that Chilean capitalists should be involved in the company, and added as an afterthought in a memorandum which has survived, 'and the bourgeois public'. In order to resist the strong and increasing tendency towards the nationalisation of public utility services, a sale of £350,000 worth of bonds in 1925 was quickly taken up in Santiago. An idea was also discussed for selling the Chilena to a group that was ostensibly Spanish but German underneath. The Foreign Office made clear its opposition to this plan, but also tipped off Pearson's that GEC were installing electricity in Athens, and added 'It might be that the system would be suitable for Santiago.'

When Tonkin announced his intention of retiring as general manager in 1926, Clive sent him a characteristically generous cable saying 'Sincerely hope health is not the cause, equally that it in no way arises from any differences with myself or other colleagues. I need hardly say I confidently hope that our friendship built on your devoted services to our common interests will continue for many a year.' Sadly, it was not to be. The month before, Clive and Alicia had entertained Tonkin and his wife and daughter for a weekend at Parham, when, he had written, 'we shall be alone except that on the Sunday a party of 15 is coming to luncheon, consisting, I think I may say, of England's most famous architects: although they will only make a flying visit of inspection I think you would find them interesting to meet.' This was the Surveyors' Club, and apart from the invaluable Victor Heal, it included Lutyens and Clough Williams-Ellis. Eight months later, in March 1927, Tonkin wrote encouragingly to Clive:

I am optimistic . . . The present government seems to have the best intentions . . . and wish to suppress a good deal of corruption which has prevailed. It seems that our upper class has failed in the administration of the country. The military believe that anyone in connection with politics in the past is marked with a stigma. They are also carrying out quite a house cleaning as far as the communists are concerned. Lots of them who have given us so much trouble have been deported.

It is worth mentioning that Russian-trained agents, even at this date, were seeking to sow the seeds of world revolution in several South American countries including Chile, and that Tonkin's words were no exaggeration. But under a rapid succession of new Presidents, each with the military strong man (and future dictator) Ibañez behind him, this forecast proved misleading, and in September Tonkin was told by the new Minister of the Interior to stop meddling in the electricity companies, on pain of being deported to the island of Juan Fernandez, formerly the abode of Robinson Crusoe but an unsatisfactory base for a senior Santiago engineer.

Ironically, just as Tonkin's own successful press campaign had played an important part in bringing about the increase in the electricity tariff in 1925, so now, two years later, the situation was reversed, partly at least through a long report to Ibañez by a journalist called Carlos Pinto Duran. Ibañez was now President, and his regime, in a nutshell, was to be characterised by suppression of the liberal political opposition and by censorship. Duran was no doubt eager to show how useful he could be to the new regime, and his report made many complaints against the Chilena: it had arranged for a government decree in 1925 'doubling, for no reason, (sic) the tramway tariff'. It had (and this was true) a far more favourable position than its opposite number in Buenos Aires, which was bound to return all its installations and other possessions to the city at the termination of its lease, whereas the municipality of Santiago merely had the right to buy them back. He went so far as to describe the company as 'a second Eiffel Tower, erected to satisfy plutocratic arrogance . . . as free from taxes as the Pharaohs of Egypt, the Emperors of China or the Tsars of Russia'. And he complained that it had 'an inhuman monopoly which would not be tolerated in any civilised country', and for good measure that 'the high voltage current was transmitted through defective installations which were a mortal danger to the inhabitants of Santiago'. Finally, 'in the absence of proper accountability a river of gold was flowing out of Chile into Europe'. In the light of all this, he recommended a general reduction in the electric light tariff, and an undertaking by the Chilena to make an investment of £4m to improve the tram system over the next four years.

What Duran failed to mention, since it did not help his case, was that the 'Illustrious Municipality of Santiago' (which, however illustrious, had never been able to establish itself on a financial footing that would permit modern public utilities which were now beginning to be taken for granted elsewhere) now owed the Chilena, according to Mr Worswick, no less than 4,800,000 pesos; and in the following April it unilaterally lowered the tariff payable on electric power. In August the government declared Don Samuel Claro, the Chilena's chief legal adviser and a member of its board, *persona non grata*, and told Pearson's that his presence on boards, or even in an advisory capacity, would prevent it from dealing with them. Claro had actually served in four of the short-lived cabinets appointed by President Alessandri between 1921 and 1924, but the legal bureau which he had created with other members of his family 'was known to his enemies, who were quite a few, as Ali Baba's Cave'.

That all this was a classic case of political pressure was confirmed a year later when the board of the Chilena received a telegram from Clive suggesting that Claro should be reappointed legal adviser to the company following fresh political developments. The general manager was then summoned first by the Minister of Finance and later by the Prime Minister, Balmaceda, himself, who told him that 'although it was not the Government's policy to interfere with the appointment of personnel in private corporations, he felt the earlier resolution concerning Sr. Claro should be kept'. This appears to have been the last straw which precipitated Clive's resignation as Chairman in January 1929. Also of interest is the reaction of Don Agostin Edwards, the owner of *El Mercurio*, the Chilean equivalent of *The Times*. He was a very senior public figure in Chile, who had been Chilean Ambassador in London from 1910 to 1924, and returned there in voluntary exile under the Ibañez regime. He was by this time a close personal friend of the Pearsons, and Cowdray Park had been lent to him on more than one occasion. Shortly before returning to Chile, he replied most engagingly to an invitation to spend a shooting weekend at Parham, 'Would you mind if I came on Saturday instead of Friday? I cannot shoot, not only because I have forgotten how to but because I have sent my guns out to Chile. Though in diplomacy we are sometimes called on to do more difficult things than shoot without guns I am afraid that having given up my post I have lost that ability . . .!', and writing to thank Alicia afterwards, he wrote: 'I do hope that next time you come to Chile you will stay with us. We cannot offer you a Parham, for there is none to be had out there, but at least you will be more comfortable than at that wretched place which has the cheek of styling itself the Savoy Hotel!' The letter that he wrote to Clive when he heard the news of Claro's ostracism is a straw in the wind that was to blow Pearsons out of Chile in the following year. It is worth quoting in full.

My dear Clive,
  Words fail me to express how indignant I feel with the Government of my country for their unspeakable attitude towards Samuel Claro, one of the very best men that we have in Chile. Their action is unworthy of any civilised government, and not only does it show the intention of treating your company unfairly by

removing the man who knew best how to defend its interests but establishes a fatal precedent, for it opens the road to Government interference in the private affairs of every firm or individual.

My hope is that men who use the power of government in this way cannot be tolerated for very long by their fellow citizens, for every one in turn will be menaced . . . but I have as great faith in the future as I have little in the present. I cannot believe that everyone in Chile has gone mad or turned into a knave! I shall make a point of going to London to meet Mr. Claro on his arrival there on the 12th of next month.

I am sure you must be very anxious about all this. The only ray of hope is that the commission they have appointed to deal with your company is composed of decent men . . . It does sometimes happen that one finds a gold coin in the sewage! Lucky man!

Yours very sincerely

AGOSTIN EDWARDS

Pearson's services to the British Government and the Admiralty had not been forgotten, and in the difficulties which were now coming to a head for the company in Chile Clive must have been pleased to receive a letter from the Foreign Office in March 1928, the writer of which had been 'directed by Sir Austen Chamberlain (the Foreign Secretary) to inform you that a telegram has been dispatched to H. M. Representative in Santiago requesting him to maintain close contact with Mr Worswick and to lend your Company all such unofficial support as he properly can'. This may have been good for morale, but later in the year Worswick, a tough American engineer who was the new general manager of the Chilena, and who must have been appointed with Tonkin's approval or even perhaps at his suggestion, wrote him the following exasperated letter which nevertheless indicates that at this stage the company still had no hard feelings against him personally.

Juan Tonkin, Esq.,   Oct. 25, 1928
Santiago,
Chile.

Dear Mr. Tonkin:

A word of explanation is due to you regarding the sale of our Chilean electrical interests to the Electric Bond and Share Company.

I need not review the details of the history of our relations with the Municipality of Santiago and with the Central Government for you, more than anyone else are familiar with our unfortunate experience, but I would like to put on record in general terms what you already know. We hoped to become *permanently* identified with the development of your country, and therefore we invited, and gave every opportunity and encouragement to Chilean capital to come in with us on the same basis as ourselves. We naturally thought the important bearing our enterprise would have on the welfare and prosperity of the country would be understood, but this unfortunately did not prove to be the case. As you know we went into the business in the most open handed and generous spirit and we hoped to get, and had every right to expect the help, encouragement and cooperation of the authorities. Instead we have experienced constant opposition amounting at times almost to persecution.

When you negotiated the 1925 contract, we thought that at last the authorities had realised their error, and we hoped our path would be smoother, but what happened – we lived up to the letter of this agreement, spent 16,000,000 pesos in giving Santiago the finest street lighting system in the world, and the municipality on their part have not paid a centavo for the street lighting service since 1925, nor did they live up to other obligations which they undertook, such as the regulation of the Bus service. They brought an iniquitous law action against us, inspired solely by bad faith, merely to avoid meeting their obligations. The culmination of this campaign of persecution was reached last year during Mr. Balmaceda's term of office, when he attacked the Company and endeavored to impose tariffs and conditions which would have spelled ruin not only to the Company but to the electrical industry in general in Chile.

The virtual expulsion of our director and lawyer Mr. Claro, for no other reason than that he was defending the interests of the Company, and the threat to your good self which compelled you to relinquish your duties, and also the threat to expel and ruin Mr. Del Rio which Mr. Balmaceda made to me personally, solely because he also was doing his duty in defending the Company, forced me to come to the conclusion that we were not wanted in Chile. On top of all this, when I came to an agreement with the Government on the question of tariffs and other matters in dispute, which I hoped would end our difficulties, no sooner had I left the country than this arrangement in a large part was repudiated.

Do you wonder that when the Americans made us an offer, we were glad to take it? If the Government and the Municipality had given us the encouragement we deserved, and which also was in their own interests to give, we would never have sold out without their full consent for we would have been in honor bound to continue to work with them. Therefore, they have only themselves to thank for our getting out of Chile.

Personally I relinquish the business without the least regret since it has caused me so much worry and trouble, but I do regret to sever the very cordial and happy relations I had with my colleagues on the boards of the Chilean and Valparaiso Companies and all other delightful Chileans I have had the pleasure of working with, who I know will also regret that we have felt compelled to take this step.

I hope that for the sake of the welfare of Chile that the authorities will treat the new owners in a different spirit than they treated us, for I know that they are animated with a sincere desire as we were, to make a success of this great public utility, and I hope that it will be realized that its success will mean prosperity also to the industrial life of Chile. It will be the policy of the new owners to try to get the Chilean public interested with them as we did, and they will naturally endeavor to work harmoniously with the authorities for the general welfare.

The Electric Bond and Share Company have asked me to help them take over the properties and I have agreed to give them some of my time off and on for the next two years. I expect to make a visit to Chile with Mr. Odlum and other representatives of his Company early next year, and the following year I will probably make another visit, and then say good-bye to Chile.

I am looking forward with pleasure to seeing Mrs. Tonkin, Ines and yourself on my forthcoming visit, and send you all kindest regards in the meantime.

Sincerely yours
A. E. WORSWICK

Clive and Alicia made several visits to Chile between 1921 and 1928, (partly because Pearson's also owned a nitrate company there) but sadly they never seem to have visited the extremely beautiful lake district in the south of the country, which they could not have failed to enjoy. At that time, however, transport was slower, the Atlantic crossing from Buenos Aires took weeks, and there was then the long journey over the Andes to Santiago. There was obviously a limit to the time that Clive wanted to spend away from headquarters in the London office. But it seems a pity that most of their time in Chile was spent in the least attractive parts of that wonderful country, though Santiago itself had at that time not been suffocated by traffic. There were also various lavish social occasions, and Alicia told her daughters with amusement that the last word in chic for ladies at the race meetings in Chile was to appear in a dress with plainly visible creases in it, to indicate that it had arrived from Paris that very morning, and had only just been unpacked. The sale of the Manson Velasco, or Velasco House, which Clive had acquired as a company headquarters, must have been particularly disappointing when Victor Heal had only just finished acquiring for it, on the spot, some delightful old Spanish furniture, pictures and tapestries, a few of which were brought back to Parham and are still to be seen in the Long Gallery.

The house, which is in a pleasant Spanish colonial style, stands on what is now a noisy crossroads on the corner of Santo Domingo and Maciver, close to the main business quarter, only a few minutes from the Cathedral and the Plaza d'Armas. It must have had great charm in days of less heavy traffic, and without the exhaust fumes which are now the abomination of the centre of the city. The outside walls were covered in dark red plaster, which contrasts rather oddly with the sky-blue walls of the nineteenth-century Gothic Colegio Rosa de Santiago over the road. It remained the residence of the general manager of the electricity company, which was later sold back to the Chileans by the Americans. Forty years later the company was nationalised under Allende and then reprivatised by Pinochet. The house was then sold off, and was opened again as a Museum of the Army in April 1990. The charming inner courtyard still looks much as it did in the large photograph album prepared for the Pearsons when they had finished decorating it.

Two years later, worse was to follow. In 1930 Tonkin made a claim for £23,179 as commission on the sale of the assets of the Compania National to the old Chilean Electricity Company as far back as 1920. Clive at first wrote back that 'Whitehall Securities is unable to recognise any claim either in respect of commission or otherwise', and that he was 'surprised and sorry that you should have thought fit to put it forward'. But Mr Odlum, the American purchaser of the Chilena, told Clive that Tonkin intended to sue the Chilena and that 'in his pleadings and trial he will wash a lot of dirty linen which will be of harm to us in Chile'. Although he cannot really have had anything to lose except Odlum's good will, Clive honourably decided in December 1930 (at a particularly troublesome time for the group, in the middle of the slump) to pay £10,000 as Whitehall Securities' share in buying off Tonkin, with Odlum paying a further £10,000 in full settlement of £20,000. Tonkin had also received 20,000 shares in the company, and even granted the huge contribution that he had made to its success, he may be said to have done well out of his connection with the tail of the lion. But it was all a far cry from the good old days in Mexico, when no cloud ever seems to have passed over the sunny relations between the Chief and the President. A good example of the differences between the activities of father and son was the fact that Lord Cowdray would spend months on end in Mexico, and had created his empire there himself, whereas Clive would only appear for brief visits in Chile, usually when some difficult decision had to be made on the spot. Later, in 1931, the American buyers of the company would themselves run into further severe difficulties caused not only by the slump but by the rise of a new dictator, the left-wing Colonel Marmaduque Grove, whose name would have been more appropriate among Clive's shooting guests at Parham than at the head of a revolutionary government in Chile. But as in Mexico after 1920, it was now for a US company to solve the problems that had lain below the surface of what had looked like an attractive acquisition. Once again, the

Pearson sense of timing had been faultless. The present Lord Cowdray, then aged eighteen, remembers being taken aside by Clive who explained to him in a state of some concern, if not embarrassment, that all the Pearson electrical companies in North and South America were to be disposed of, and feared that the future heir would resent this reduction of the family empire. However, Clive added that there were circumstances in which it would be advisable to sell one's own grandmother if the price were right; and his nephew accepted Clive's decision, which turned out to have been a thoroughly wise one, without demur. The price obtained from the American and Foreign Power Co. for Whitehall Securities' Mexican interests were just under £14m and that of the interests in Chile was £2.25m.

Four years after the sale of the Chilena, there was to be a curious sequel. In 1932, Clive suddenly heard from Valparaiso that the Chilean Government had decided to honour him with its highest civil decoration and make him Gran Oficial de la Orden al Merito, the highest grade except for the Grand Cross, which in recent years had only been conferred on the Prince of Wales. The first letter stated that the order was granted

> as a testimony of the gratitude of the Chilean Government for your initiative in the development of the electric industry in Chile ... they consider it is due to your initiative and the investment of a very large capital in this industry that the country has been able to enjoy enormous industrial benefits. It is due entirely to your good friend Don Pedro Torres (now General Manager of the Bank of Chile) that the results of your energies have been kept before the Powers that be, so that the honour and credit of such great undertakings go to where they are due.

The Chilean Ambassador in London wrote to the Foreign Secretary for approval of Clive's acceptance, but according to him the decoration was in recognition of the construction of the port of Valparaiso, and not of the installation of the electricity supply. The solution of this contradiction may be that the new President Allessandri, who had recently succeeded Grove, was now particularly keen to repair, if possible, the confidence of foreign (and especially British) investors which had been badly shaken by the consequences of the dictatorship of Ibañez between 1925 and 1931. Restricted permission was given to Clive by the King, following the usual protocol, to wear the decoration on occasions connected with Chile. Clive wrote a characteristically self-effacing and generous letter to Sir Ernest Moir, who had originally been in charge of the port construction, saying that while the decoration had fallen to him, the honour belonged to Sir Ernest, together with Mr A. C. Walsh and Mr Ernest Pearson.

The Great Hall, Castle Fraser and BELOW *the Library, with original bookcases and wallpaper of about 1839.*

Views of Castle Fraser in the 1920s.

Parham: the restored Elizabethan south front.

The Great Hall, rearranged with new acquisitions.

ABOVE *Toby Fitzwilliam.* BELOW *Eugenie Godfrey-Faussett and Alicia, Madeira 1935.*

ABOVE *Clive's brother and sister-in-law, Lord and Lady Cowdray.* BELOW *Relief of Victor Heal in New Change.*

ABOVE *The Bus Service, Athens, March 1938.* BELOW *Outside the hotel at Olympia. Alicia and Clive back right; Sir Gerald Talbot in dressing gown, next to Veronica; the Mayor of Athens seated right, the Minister of Finance seated centre.*

 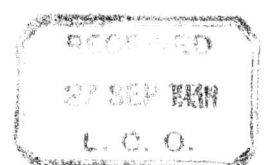

10, Downing Street,
Whitehall,

25th September 1938.

Dear Mr Pearson,

Now that I have returned from my second visit to Herr Hitler, I feel that I must write and thank you for the excellent travelling arrangements made by British Airways. On both occasions, and especially on the second, the flight in each direction was accomplished with an ease and rapidity which I, as an inexperienced air-traveller, had not previously thought possible. I am very grateful for the pains taken by your Company to ensure the speed, safety and comfort of my journeys, and I hope that you will convey my thanks to all those who by their efforts contributed to these ends.

Yours sincerely,

Neville Chamberlain

The Hon. Clive Pearson.

Neville Chamberlain on return from his second visit to Hitler, September 1938.
OPPOSITE *The Prime Minister's letter to Clive thanking him for British Airways' travelling arrangements.*

Clive's three daughters:
RIGHT *Dione*
BELOW, LEFT *Veronica*
BELOW, RIGHT *Lavinia*

5
Life between the Wars

The story of Clive's life indicates how invariably he lived by the family motto, 'Do it with thy might', already mentioned.

Apart from the group of companies in Chile, he had of course been concerned with a host of other business projects undertaken by Whitehall Securities in the 1920s. First, there were extensive searches for oil all over the world. As early as January 1918 Lord Murray of Elibank, who was a director of Pearson's but had also been Secretary of State at the India Office in 1909, wrote to one of his former colleagues there that 'the British Empire is almost entirely dependent on foreign oil, and Lord Cowdray is laying plans for a serious attempt to develop oil *in* the Empire, including India'. Europe was still in the turmoil of war, Russia was convulsed with revolution; United States policy was quite unpredictable, and South America still a largely unknown quantity. The best hope of self-sufficiency in oil, the life-blood of future national security, lay in a great imperial scheme. There had been discussions on the possible amalgamation of Mexican Eagle with the Anglo-Persian and Burmah Oil Companies to form a vast, truly British controlled group. But Cowdray felt that his responsibilities to such a large concern would be excessive, and that he would become tied to it permanently and inextricably, to the detriment of all the other interests that he had developed over the years, including family and charitable enterprises: 'I and my sons', he wrote, 'would have to remain for an indefinite period in the oil business, whereas today we are free to clear out whenever we want.' The extremely successful way in which they did so has already been set out in the previous chapter.

By April 1921 there were plans to drill oil wells not only in India, but in Trinidad, Egypt and Morocco, and to acquire land in Canada. Over £2m had been spent on these schemes by the end of 1922, from the proceeds of the sale of Mexican Eagle to Royal Dutch. Pearson's also made unsuccessful attempts in France, all over Eastern Europe, in Iraq, and in many places in the Far East, including China. Clive may not have been directly involved in the details, but as chairman of Whitehall Petroleum after 1923 he had ultimate responsibility for them, and their repeated failure, generally as a result of national suspicions in the post-war atmosphere of ever-increasing independence from the former influence of the Great Powers (not unlike those which had led to Pearson's undoing in Chile) must have been a source of disappointment and concern. Two sharply contrasting efforts were with companies formed to operate in the USA, Amerada and Rycade, which harnessed the store of experience built up by Mexican Eagle in the years of triumph, and were run by directors and staff who were loyally determined to remain within the Pearson empire.

Amerada was incorporated in 1920, for tax reasons in the state of Delaware, and its original capital was increased to $6m in 1922. Whitehall Petroleum owned over 60% of the stock, and there were about fifty other shareholders. In 1921, its first full year of operating, the company produced 1,726,353 barrels of oil, chiefly in Oklahoma, Kansas and Texas, and the figure rose to 5,659,370 barrels in 1926. In that year, however, it became necessary to allow the US shareholdings to outnumber the British ones, if the company was to own land legally in Texas. However, this involved great advantages, for in 1927 the production almost doubled, to a figure in excess of ten million barrels. The directors were all old Aguila hands, Body, Carr, Ryder and de Golyer, and they and members of their families were also among the individual shareholders. Their remuneration was fixed at 2½% of profits, and as these rose from 1,198,873 in 1921 to $4,933,083 in 1926, they must have become rich men. In 1926 40% of the shares owned outside the USA were sold to an American company called Dillon, Read, at $20 a share. Whitehall Securities sold 148,744 out of the 361,383 that they owned for a figure of $611,564. The company also became advanced in research into the new science of geophysics, and as well as the advantages that this gave them in its own explorations, its geophysical department was also constantly in demand for carrying out research for other oil companies in areas in which Amerada was not active. Curiously enough, small finds of oil were also made nearer home, among other places in Derbyshire, and a photograph survives of Lord Cowdray and Lord and Lady Hartington, probably taken in 1919, inspecting a trickle emerging from the ground in the neighbourhood of Chatsworth. Oil was one of the chief spheres in which Pearson's had successful experience, and apart from the prodigious success achieved in America (which continues to this day, since the

Pearson group still owns Camco, a profitable business which makes valves for use in oil extraction in Texas) oil had to be pursued seriously in other parts of the world.

Amerada's role was to develop oil interests in Canada, and in the United States with the exception of the state of Texas, where state law required that the majority of shares in any operating company should be in American hands. The Rycade company was therefore formed to operate exclusively in Texas, and it took its name from the first two letters of the names of the oil experts who ran it, Ryder, Carr and De Golyer, all of whom were Americans. To meet the requirements of the law, the share capital was owned by the American directors, and the loan capital by Pearson's. For many years it was far and away the least successful of all the companies in which Pearson's ever held a stake, and it was fortunate that they only held 49% of the shares. The only year between 1928 and 1936 in which it made a loss of less than $1m was 1935, and that was because it succeeded in that year in selling a 240-acre lease for a total of $960,000, thereby exactly halving the loss for the year. In other years the losses ranged from $1.258m in 1933 to over $2m in 1928. Lord Cowdray remained in close touch with what was going on and actually made a visit to Texas in 1927, the year before his death. At that time the total deficit was $4m, against assets of $1.7m. The company owned 80 dry or 'lost' holes, as against 42 wells that had been successfully 'brought in'. Allegedly, to close down the company altogether would have cost more than to endure the huge annual losses. These had in reality been caused by the company having, uncharacteristically, rushed in and bought land because of the 'general impression that there would be few if any good prospects left in a few years'. By December 1928 Clive was writing to De Golyer that 'the company's future is still a gamble, with the dice loaded against us by the large amount of money expended to date'.

It must also be remembered that in the worst days of the depression the price of oil fell within a short space of time from $1 a barrel to 10 cents a barrel. Rycade had a bonded debt of about $3 million, but as it was owed to Pearson's own bankers nothing would have been gained by foreclosing on it. Oil prices recovered in the 1930s and a Mr Bouvier was appointed to run the company, which he did with much success. Soon after Clive's retirement, Lord Cowdray and Oliver Poole decided to re-enter the oil market, and by that time Rycade was making such large profits that within four years it had paid the purchase price of another oil company called initially Progress Petroleum, later renamed Midhurst Oil. Later still, in 1970, most of Midhurst Oil, with which Rycade had merged, was sold to Ashland Oil in Kentucky, with the exception of 100,000 acres of mineral and surface rights scattered round the United States, which did not suit Ashland geographically. Many of them were in fact old Rycade properties, and as recently as 1989 the remains of these holdings were sold for a further $64 million. The happy ending of this story only came about many years after Clive's death, but his faith in the company, and his patience in holding onto something that had lost huge sums of money year after year was abundantly justified. Ironically, the company had not really been intended by the first Lord Cowdray to make money for Pearson's but to reward Ryder, Carr and de Golyer and make them financially secure in return for having been instrumental in making such a vast fortune in oil for him in the first place.

Soon after this time Cowdray decided that the contracting business that had first made his fortune was becoming increasingly competitive, and for it to be as successful as it had originally been it would need his own undivided attention; it may well have been that he did not see, among his subordinates, anyone capable of the prodigious, single-minded efforts that he had put into it himself. With the exception of the Sennar Dam project, which was not finished till 1925, he therefore decided to close down. He might well have sold it off to a competitor, or turned it into a public company, run by other people, but he was unwilling to let the firm that bore his name, and that owed virtually everything to his own industry, integrity and vision, to fall into other hands. Some thought this a foolish decision, but it is hard to think of any other man who had better earned the right to please himself over the future of his own creation. The subsequent diversification of the group, largely under Clive's ultimate management, now meant, in the word's of Cowdray's official biographer, that 'the course of events was gradually transforming his organisation into a great Investment Trust, controlling and directing numerous enterprises at home and abroad, which would need all his time and thought, and that of his sons and partners'. One important field of activity was the group of regional electrical companies which were acquired and developed in England by Whitehall Electric, chiefly in Devon and Somerset. These too were naturally built on solid foundations, by means of the experience gained in the ancillary works attached to the great contracting schemes of the past.

Clive was a dutiful and obedient son, and there is no record of his having hankered after a policy of preserving and developing still further the old traditional glories of S. Pearson & Son, Contractors. (He was not even on the board of the contracting department of Pearson's). The business world of the 1920s, stricken though it was by so much death and destruction, was a forward-looking one. Many pre-war notions soon came to be looked on as out of date, and all through the years between the wars, Clive was correspondingly on the lookout for fresh fields to conquer, and modern inventions and utilities to invest in. The world had changed, the 'Old Gang' was discredited in the country, and there was to be no looking back, especially for those who had plenty of money in the bank for new projects. However, the general methods were to be the same as before: sensible use of past experience as a basis from which to move forward; painstaking research and costing; and above all, complete integrity, and an insistence on the highest standards, with an unflagging example set from the top.

Another electrical venture, in which over £½m was invested in 1930, was the Fuerzas Motrices del Valle de Lecrin in South-Eastern Spain. This company, which was on the same lines as the Chilean group, but smaller, made worthwhile profits between 1931 and 1935, but large losses followed in the next two years as a result of the Civil War, and the area was actually bombarded by the German Navy in 1937. Whitehall Securities received a satisfactory return on its investment in the early years, but the company was finally sold to an American group in 1942. Clive was not on the board of the Spanish company, but since it affected Whitehall Securities it was yet another source of concern to him at a difficult time. It would be tedious to go into the technical details of all these operations, since this is not a history of the Pearson group, but Clive inevitably devoted much time and trouble to them when the need arose.

Another company, which was to have a longer and more successful history, was the Athens Piraeus Electricity Co., already referred to. Again, Clive was not on the board himself, but remained ultimately responsible through his position as chairman of Whitehall Electric, and there is evidence to show how very careful he was to prevent the same kind of trouble arising as had been the case in Chile. By 1936 the Greek company was able to look back on ten years of solid achievement in developing a satisfactory domestic and industrial supply in what had, by European standards, been a backward capital city as far as public utilities were concerned. It published an elegant report, bound in brown suede, which said that 'Pearson's had contributed the technical experience of special collaborators', as well as abundant capital, both for installations, indemnifications and expropriations. Street lighting had been introduced, as in Santiago; and also floodlighting of ancient monuments, statues, fountains, avenues and modern buildings as well; a supply was also created for agricultural and industrial consumers, and finally a domestic supply for all at a low tariff. Consumption in Athens itself rose from 27.5 kilowatts in 1925 to 110 million, and the number of individual consumers increased from 14,000 to 121,000.

Of course, there were criticisms of the same kind as those in Chile, and there were murmurings that 'Pearson's were a power within a power'. The left-wing newspaper *Hestia* complained that as a result of the continuous increase in the consumption of electricity, production expenses had risen to a level intolerable for a country as poor as Greece. Hydro-electric schemes had been neglected, 'the ever lucrative operation of which should have been one of the principal sources of municipal revenue'. But as in the case of the Athens-Piraeus Railway, they blamed the government, which was more fun than blaming the contracting company. Another paper, *Typos*, conceded a wide measure of success, and added that although 'the Electricity Co. has made us drink many a bitter cup', it could redress the wrongs for which it was responsible, provided the will was there. As well as the normal electricity and tramways, Pearson's also had a share in the bus company, and Clive paid several visits to Athens, one of them for an enjoyable anniversary celebration. He took particular pleasure in the company of Leslie Kemp, who was managing director of the Athens office, and of other colleagues including Thomas Bloomfield and David Pawson. The Greek connection established by Pearson's also led, as will be seen, to a great benefit to the Greeks in London when the war came and 32 Grosvenor Square became the focal point of their community.

Other companies were acquired from time to time in the 1930s, too numerous to list here. But mention should be made of one of the most successful, the Acton Bolt Co., which was formed to exploit a patent for the production of a self-locking thread bolt. When it was finally sold to GKN nearly thirty years later in 1962, it was one of the largest makers of high tensile nuts and bolts in the country. More seriously, Lazards were beset by a multitude of problems in 1931. Apart from the general conditions of the slump and the devaluation of the dollar, the firm had lent sterling to the Austrian Credit Anstalt, which was controlled by the Rothschild family but had been surprisingly mismanaged and now collapsed. No less than a hundred other foreign banks were also involved as creditors and were now asked to agree to a moratorium on repayments.

Fortunately Lazards were not among the major creditors, but far worse was to come. In 1920 they had opened an office an Antwerp, followed by a second office in Brussels under a Czech manager called Vithek, whose instructions were to deal exclusively in foreign exchange. Lazards in London now however heard that excessively high rates were being offered by Vithek for short money, and the reason turned out to be that he had gone far beyond his brief and had been incurring very heavy losses on the Brussels Stock Market, which he was staving off by means of repeated short borrowings. He was also keeping two sets of books of account, only one of which was shown to the auditors. Vithek died suddenly on the Friday when the position became known to Lazards in London, but the office was somehow opened on the Monday morning as if nothing had happened. Both the Brussels and Antwerp offices were however closed as soon as possible, but to regularise Lazards' position the Bank of England required Pearson's (which in effect meant Clive and his brother) to increase their deposits if Lazards were to be allowed to continue operating as an issuing house. Both Lord Kindersley and M. André Mayer later stated their intense gratitude to Clive for organising this support, in return for which Pearson's stake in Lazards now rose to 83%. But the other details of this traumatic affair are one of the best-kept secrets of the traditional world of merchant banking. After the general recovery of the overall position of Pearson's, in the mid 1930s when the slump was over, another blow fell, which in a sense had been foreseen by Clive's father when he sold control of Mexican Eagle in 1920. This was the expropriation of foreign-owned assets in Mexico in 1938 by the Cardenas government, which in the previous year had ordered the oil companies to pay higher wages. This with great reluctance they had agreed to do. But they were also instructed to train Mexican employees for promotion to responsible positions, which was not unreasonable in view of the way in which they had been literally draining the country's natural resources for over thirty years. The companies refused, and the oilfields were summarily handed over to a government corporation, with most of the managerial positions being given to former trade union officials, with a highly predictable loss of efficiency. In revenge, the companies boycotted Mexican oil and made it difficult for Mexico to obtain tankers of her own.

The trouble really went back to the days of President Diaz, who in his eagerness for industrial development had failed to protect the interests of the Mexicans themselves, or to insist that they should learn the new techniques introduced by foreign entrepreneurs. In companies like Mexican Eagle, foreigners monopolised every responsible position and the Mexicans were only employed as unskilled labour. It is easy, and not unreasonable, to criticise this, but how long would it have taken, in those primitive days, to train them for higher things? It should not be forgotten that when natural resources on this scale are suddenly discovered, whether oil in Mexico or gold and diamonds in South Africa, human greed brings about an intense spirit of competition, and from the purely commercial point of view speed and efficiency are everything. Unlike some of the American bosses, with whom Cowdray himself was in fierce competition, the Mexican Eagle managers did not shoot down Mexican workers who struck for higher pay. They paid them more highly in the first place, and took trouble to see to their welfare, health and education, in so far as the Mexicans themselves were willing. It was the ruthless greed of the Americans that sowed the seed for the regular crop of revolutions that followed between 1911 and 1920, and as Evelyn Waugh was to observe, the Americans' attitude to Mexico had been that of the nineteenth-century Englishman towards Ireland. And however enlightened Pearsons' policy towards their workers may have been, especially by comparison with that of others, the system already settled between the American oil pioneers and Diaz included the manifest injustice that apart from a negligible stamp duty the owners of oil in Mexico paid no taxes there and could export it as they liked. For twenty-five years Diaz tolerated no rivals near his throne, and he does not appear to have cared what would happen when he died. Inevitably, the interested parties jockeyed for position in what was to become deadly earnest.

To return to 1938: Cardenas broke off diplomatic relations with Britain after an angry British protest, but more importantly Roosevelt's government in Washington recognised the expropriation as legitimate, provided proper compensation was paid, and this was naturally of great psychological importance in helping to remove the sense of national inferiority and the hostility to foreigners which had been the fruits of the Diaz regime. Compensation was eventually agreed with the US companies before Pearl Harbour, but it was not till 1947 that the British companies received a total of £7.5m.

Clive was evidently so incensed by the principle of expropriation that he made his only foray into the world of literature, and commissioned Evelyn Waugh, who was at that time as well known for his travel writings as for his novels, to go to Mexico and write a book about it. Sadly, no correspondence between them or other details have survived, except in a letter from Waugh, whose wife had contracted appendicitis in Mexico but was only operated on after their return to England. He wrote to his agent A. D. Peters 'Poor Laura was operated on. Does Uncle Clive's insurance still stand?', referring to the health insurance which had covered the trip itself. No answer is recorded. The book was called *Robbery under Law*, and though perhaps the least successful of all his works is naturally more readable than the best books of any number of other authors. It is not a reliable or even balanced account of Mexico. It is written from a rigidly conservative standpoint, and though the author was of course sharply observant he was above all concerned, as a robust convert to the Catholic Church, with what had been its severe persecution in Mexico. He admits at the beginning of the book that it is primarily political, and not much concerned with travel. A cheap edition was published in 1940, the year after its first publication, but by that time the attention of most readers had been distracted from the troubles of Mexico. Waugh certainly later had a low opinion of the book, and probably only took on the commission because he had recently married and had no regular means of supporting a wife and children. He did not allow it to be reprinted in the collected edition of his works. Nevertheless it contains many points of interest, such as the announcements made by the oil companies in public advertisements that they would not obey the decisions of the Supreme Court of Mexico, and would not be responsible for what happened to the country, which of course impugned the position of the President. Waugh also concedes that Cardenas had used his influence in 1936 to bring the persecution of the Church to an end, and when the expropriations took place, the Church allowed collections to be taken up at its doors to go towards the national debt that was being incurred on compensation. He also makes the point that the oil companies, and especially perhaps Shell, had paid high wages, and latterly high taxes. It was hardly their fault if the workmen misspent the wages and the politicians misspent the taxes as well as the bribes without which nothing connected with official life could ever be brought about.

One of the chief new recruits to the groups in the 1930s was Robin Gurdon, who married Clive's niece Yoskyl in 1932, and whose death in action in Libya in 1942 was a particularly severe loss to his brother-in-law Lord Cowdray as well as to the rest of his family. He would undoubtedly have played a major part in the group's progress after the war had he survived it, and an interesting notebook that he kept in 1938 was preserved by Clive, and contains some valuable details not easily accessible elsewhere. In an analysis of Whitehall Electric's deployment of its resources at the time, he shows that 25% of its funds were invested in an American company concerned with ventures in Peru and Chile; 27% in Central Europe, mainly in Germany; and of the remaining 48%, nearly a third was in oil, a quarter was invested in gilt-edged stock, awaiting some future application, and the remainder in railways in Britain, and in breweries and industrial shares. Robin Gurdon also looked ahead in an interesting fashion, and among his notes is the reflection that 'Today the question for the Treasury is "How far can we go with taxation?", but tomorrow it will be "How far can we go with inflation?", owing to the crippling burden of rearmament, even at the pace that had then been reached. Another interesting point was his prediction that in the General Election that would have been held in 1940, but for the war and the formation of a National Government, Labour would win. He also records that in 1939 the idea of agricultural investment in Kenya was carefully considered by the group, but was in the end rejected by Clive, on the general grounds that it would add to the total of investments that were locked up in cold storage and not easily, let alone profitably, realised if changing circumstances should make it desirable to do so.

The family's home life at Parham and in London has been vividly chronicled by Clive's daughter Lavinia in her book *A Nice Clean Plate*, which gave much pleasure to all who were in any way connected with it, as is shown by the letters that she received from former employees and others who had personal experience of the story. But it is sad to read how apprehensive the children appear to have felt about life, in spite of loving their parents deeply, and being protected, though not over-protected, on every side. Veronica nevertheless apparently suffered from a surprising fear that there were, or might be, foxes lurking in the chimney of her bedroom in London. But irrational fears are common enough in children, and it would be wrong to read too much into their anxieties. The children all enjoyed being read aloud to, and later reading for themselves, and also hiding in the spacious cupboards of Grosvenor Square.

Alicia naturally played much the larger part in the childhood of her daughters. Lavinia recalled her gift for reading aloud, in an exceptionally soft and attractive voice, which was much in demand especially if members of the family or friends were ill in bed, but also all through the girls' early childhood. One gushing acquaintance told Alicia that her voice was 'like an Irish legend', which led to a good deal of subsequent teasing. Favourite books for reading aloud included the Fairy Books of Andrew Lang – Pink, Red and Blue – and the works of Mrs Molesworth and Frances Hodgson Burnett, in particular *The Secret Garden*. Kipling was also favoured, but Mowgli rather than the *Just So Stories*, which the children hated. Dickens and Hardy were attempted, but proved too sad, but Edward Lear, Harry Graham and Lewis Carroll were much enjoyed, together with a wide variety of assorted poetry. Both Alicia and her mother had a talent for inventing stories and adding their own improvisations. Clive was fond of *The Wind in the Willows*, and occasionally compared himself cheerfully to the ebullient Mr Toad, rushing about the countryside in his Rolls-Royce, though it is not easy to see any striking similarity at this distance of time. He also liked Surtees, but more surprisingly, he greatly enjoyed the gossamer threads of Logan Pearsall Smith's *Trivia*, and this was perhaps another example of his taking recommendations from acknowledged experts, in this case Alicia, on trust.

As a child, Alicia herself had attended classes in London given by the remarkable Miss Woolf, where one of her fellow pupils was Vita Sackville-West. When the weekly essays were handed back, Miss Woolf would always say 'Vita's was the best, of course', but as it was never read out, the other pupils could only admire and imagine. Another fellow pupil was Louise of Battenberg, whose brother later became Lord Mountbatten. She and Alicia worked together in 1914 at the Soldiers' and Sailors' Families Association, and she later married the King of Sweden. Her husband was a dedicated archaeologist, and in later life would take an annual holiday digging on sites in Italy. The Queen would then pay a visit to England and always saw her old friends from Miss Woolf's, including 'Dearest Sloper', a childhood nickname for Alicia with which the Queen invariably began her many letters to her. When she first visited Parham some special pillow-cases were brought out, inherited from Clive's mother, and so impressively coroneted and fringed with lace that they were not normally used. In fact they proved to be so heavily embroidered that the Queen found them impossible to sleep on, and asked for something plainer and smoother. She sometimes stayed at the Hyde Park Hotel, and would go out alone on shopping expeditions. But in case she might faint or be run over, she kept in her handbag a large sheet of paper saying 'I am the Queen of Sweden', though the likelihood of this being believed cannot have been strong. Later, when Alicia's son-in-law

Michael Smiley was in a prison camp in Germany, the Queen sent him priceless Red Cross parcels of food and other comforts, including selections from the King's cast-off underclothes. More unconventionally, Alicia had also spent a short time at Studleigh Agricultural College in her youth, and was able to surprise her children with quite a wide knowledge of the secrets of milking cows and keeping bees, and of the rigours of lambing.

But on the whole, life at 32 Grosvenor Square was conventional and steady. Clive's hair was regularly cut in the morning, before he went to the office, by a barber who appeared at the house at 8 a.m. His chauffeur, Mr Petre, would sigh deeply at the shortcomings of passing motorists, and exclaim despondently 'Owner driver! What can you expect?' But in spite of – or because of – the prevailing luxury any true independence or spontaneity was usually impossible. As Lavinia neatly put it, to be able to say 'We shall be eighteen for lunch and twenty-four for dinner' has its advantages, but you could never say 'I won't have anything to eat until I'm hungry' or 'Dinner will be at midnight', as the servantless inhabitants of the modern world can do to their hearts' content. The family were all part of a still elaborate system, and there was a price to be paid for enjoying its benefits.

Clive was naturally shy and ungregarious. Entertaining was done either as a social duty or as a means of lubricating the wheels of business. He startled the family circle one day by announcing that there were only three things that he felt really strongly about: music, free trade, and cooking. One of them expressed surprise about music being included. 'Oh yes', he replied, 'I'm *against* it!' Indeed, after the war, when Dione became engaged to the keenly musical Pat Gibson, whose vocal powers had been mentioned among his other qualities, her mother advised her in mock horror '*Don't* let him sing to Daddy!' When they were small, his daughters' chief experience of him was on his regular visits to the nursery to check the account books in which the expenditure of their monthly pocket money of five shillings was, according to a friend, 'unfaithfully recorded'. Only when they grew up did Clive's children become fully aware of the importance of his qualities, his fairness and conscientiousness, and his great underlying generosity. Unlike music, the theatre was a relaxation to him, at least in its more undemanding forms. The Crazy Gang were particular favourites, and Veronica recalls her father being reduced to fits of helpless laughter by the resemblance between Bud Flanagan, who was up to a point the leader of the Gang, and Cridland. His only hope of not causing a major disturbance on these occasions was to stuff a handkerchief into his mouth to stifle the gales of laughter which shook him uncontrollably. Even so, there were times when he ended up on the floor under his seat in the Victoria Palace Theatre, completely overwhelmed by the sheer fun of it all. No doubt it was a safety valve from the solemn burden of running Whitehall Securities, week in, week out, and the Cowdray Trust, and Parham and Paddockhurst, and Castle Fraser and Grosvenor Square, and all the hundred and one other exacting calls on his attention.

Apart from these occasional relaxations, Clive could be impatient with people whose minds worked less rapidly and clearly than his own. He could be gruff and stern on first acquaintance, and he sometimes enjoyed teasing people, especially his much valued friend Victor Heal. On one occasion, a guest who was sitting between them at lunch at Parham, not having taken in Victor Heal's profession, asked Clive if he knew of a good architect to carry out some work. 'I don't know about a *good* architect', was the reply. 'I don't even know if there is such a thing. But I do know someone who *is* an architect, for what it's worth, etc., etc. He's sitting next to you.' A large part of his charm evidently lay in the way he would suddenly switch from being formidable to a more light-hearted and engaging attitude in this way. He had an instinctive urge to put people to the test: if you stood up to him, and you were on firm ground, he would soon come to be friendly, while to anyone in distress or need, like Toby Fitzwilliam, his loyalty was rock-like, and his generosity very considerable. But his helpfulness went far beyond those who were in trouble, and there are many other minor examples of his consideration for various individuals who only had the sketchiest claim on his attention, as well as at least one other of large-scale personal financial help.

Parham was fully staffed. First and foremost came Cridland, with three footmen under him as well as Clive's valet; there was a housekeeper, a cook, four housemaids, two kitchenmaids, a scullery-maid and a still-room maid (in charge of jam-making and other distillations); a hall boy, an odd man, a night-watchman, and a nanny and nurserymaid to look after the girls. On the other hand, there were no labour-saving devices. But there was plenty of attention to detail. Home-made arrangements were best. In those days the tops of wine-bottles were sealed with a casing of lead, rather than with the foil of today. Under Clive's influence, Paddy Tritton later had the lead from this source carefully preserved, and when a sufficient supply had accumulated, it would be boiled down in a special saucepan and melted into paperweights and door-stops which are still in use at Parham to this day.

The children had to abide by the rules. Horses and horsemanship were considered of great importance, and Veronica, who was the keenest and best rider, came to hear of a new school called Westonbirt, where girls could take their ponies and hunt on Tuesdays with the Duke of Beaufort's hounds, provided that Tuesday's work was done on the previous Saturday. Such was her determination and persistence that she was eventually allowed to go there, no doubt to the considerable benefit of all concerned.

In 1933, after the very sudden death of his brother Harold at the early age of fifty-one, which must have come as a severe shock to him, Clive was advised by his doctor to give up polo, which he had very much enjoyed in his youth but had only had time to play intermittently since 1924. He was still only forty-six, and the phrase used by doctors and unquestioningly accepted by their patients in those days, was 'a strained heart'. Clive had been an enthusiastic and competent player, and without being brilliant he applied himself to it with the concentration that he gave to all his activities. His sister Trudie, Lady Denman, took a much more relaxed attitude to the game, and once wrote to him from Australia, where her husband was Governor-General: 'I don't often hit the ball, but I ride off with great success. They all laugh so when they see me coming that they often miss the ball too, so I feel I am a real help to my side!' Fresh air and exercise were however still highly desirable for someone who was often desk-bound like Clive, and after a somewhat half-hearted flirtation with golf, Clive became much attracted by the idea of sailing, which had so much to offer in the way of technical details. Together with his sister and her daughter Judy, he acquired The Red House, Thorpeness. Their first boat was a half-decked centreboard sailing dinghy, the *Nippy*, and the following year they hired a more substantial cabin boat called the *John Edwards* from a builder and hirer of boats at Aldeburgh, who wrote that 'with a little help from John or myself, you and Miss Lavinia and Miss Dione could get the little ship to do what you wanted and not have her way all the time'. Later there was a five-ton auxiliary sloop, the *Hind*, and in July 1935 Clive made a plan with a new sailing friend, Paddy Tritton, to sail all the way round the coast from Aldeburgh to Chichester. They had met by chance. Tritton's first wife, Judy, was searching, head first, for a dog that had disappeared into the opening of a large land drain. Clive's attention was caught by the shapely lower half of a female form backing out of the drain, and made her acquaintance on the spot.

In the last three summers before the war, sailing holidays were spent at a rented house at Bembridge in the Isle of Wight, which as well as being convenient for the Pearson aircraft interests, also offered far more attractions of a social kind to three almost grown-up daughters. Clive also suddenly developed a new taste for household shopping. He would often tie up in the harbour at Cowes and later return triumphantly with a new brand of sausages, or bread from a special baker that he had discovered. It was not an activity that had come his way before, and his family were often touched by the pleasure that it gave him.

Apart from business and the needs of Parham, social life was not neglected. Clive and Alicia may have been shy and reserved, but they threw themselves dutifully into the task of giving dances almost every year, after 32 Grosvenor Square was reopened in 1933, either for the two older girls or for god-daughters or other relations. This was done with the efficiency and attention to detail which was the hallmark of all Pearson operations. They also gave a number of dinner parties, during the season, before other dances given by friends. Alicia was always daunted by the approach of these festivities, but in the event was often seen greatly enjoying, to her surprise, the company of her neighbours at dinner when they happened to share one of her many interests and tastes and areas of knowledge. Lavinia in particular remembered the dances as being lively and thoroughly enjoyable, thanks to the mixture of the company and the predictably high standard of organisation. But she also remembered that the role of the chaperone was hard indeed. Very few fathers could be bothered to attend the dances, so the unfortunate dinner-party hostess, who usually had to stay to the end of the dance to see that the girls under her care were likely to get home safely, could find herself sitting for hours on an uncomfortable sofa, with only some probably uncongenial other women to talk to. But Alicia, in spite of considerable shyness, somehow made the best of these occasions, and even made some good friends under these unpromising circumstances. She also devised a method of stylish, if not fashionable, dressing, often in remodelled nineteenth-century ballroom clothes of Spitalfields silk or brocade found in antique shops, of a quality that would be the envy of costume museums of today.

6
Collecting Pictures and Books

Apart from the absorbing business of the alterations to the structure of the house at Parham, Clive and Alicia had also embarked, soon after their marriage, on what was to be a lifelong career as picture collectors. Antique furniture was a field that Clive and Alicia explored with characteristic thoroughness and taste, and 32 Grosvenor Square and Parham were both gradually filled with furniture that harmonised with surroundings and period. But pictures were a more abiding passion, perhaps because the difference between one oak chest and another, or one inlaid bureau and the next, is usually without the historical and personal connections of pictures, or at any rate the kind of pictures that interested them.

Their collection was gathered together, roughly speaking, in three separate categories. The first, chronologically, consisted of portraits and other pictures connected with Alicia's family. When Alicia's father had married for the second time he was not well off, and had to make provision for possible future children by selling family possessions. In 1918 Lord Cowdray, in an act of characteristic kindness and of particular imaginative goodwill towards his new daughter-in-law, bought from him a group of eighteenth-century portraits of high quality which became one of the cornerstones of the Pearsons' own collection. It contains portraits of Major Norton Knatchbull by Gainsborough, his niece Miss Joan Knatchbull by Romney, and soon afterwards other portraits by Romney of Sir Edward Knatchbull and his wife, born Mary Hugessen, whose surname was added by the Knatchbulls to their own. These were all agreeable portraits which had the extra point of commemorating members of Alicia's direct family, which would otherwise have been scattered. But the jewel of this first group was the portrait of Sir Joseph Banks by Reynolds (which may now be seen at the National Portrait Gallery). Banks had married Dorothea Hugessen, whose sister Mary, just mentioned, had married Sir Edward Knatchbull, from whom Alicia was directly descended; indeed, Alicia's third name was Dorothea, no doubt after Lady Banks; and it must certainly have been in honour of the man who was perhaps the greatest naturalist of the eighteenth century, who accompanied Captain Cook on his first voyage round the world in *Endeavour* (1768–71) and became President of the Royal Society, that Alicia planted the four magnificent Banksia roses, named after her great-great-aunt, which now reach to the full height of the south front of Parham. (His biography by Patrick O'Brian, published by Collins in 1987, is an infinitely rewarding book.)

The second category of pictures which Clive and Alicia set about collecting was of those directly connected with Parham and the families who had owned it over the centuries. The nucleus of these was a group of ninety-two pictures which the Pearsons had acquired from Lady Zouche together with the house. They included portraits of Queen Elizabeth and of Henry IV of France and Sir Philip Sidney, and later works by Kneller, Hudson and Romney. There was also a group of country-house pictures of horses and other animals and birds by Wootton, Seymour, Snyders and Hondecoete, to which Alicia added three excellent pictures of racehorses by Seymour, acquired from a dealer in Brighton; and Dutch and Italian School pictures of varying quality, together with copies of larger and more imposing works by Vandyke, Poussin and Murillo. As time went by and the Pearsons' own collection grew, inferior items were weeded out and there were a number of disposals at the sale of Paddockhurst on the death of Lady Cowdray in 1933, when Clive sold the house and one of the farms to the Benedictine order of monks, who established there a successful school, at first called Worth Priory, now Worth Abbey. Clive also kept, and moved to Parham, a group of important pictures acquired by his father between 1904 and 1922, usually either through Duveen or Agnew. These included portraits of Louis XIII and his wife Anne of Austria by Pourbus, three more Romneys, one of which, of Lady Isabella Erskine, had cost as much as £17,000 in 1904; two Vandykes, of Madame Kirk, and Marquesa de Leganez (now in the Huntingdon Harford Library in Connecticut, and Tokyo, respectively); a self-portrait by Hoppner, a portrait of Alderman Beckford by Romney, a good Raeburn of a Mrs Muir, and Sir Thomas More from the school of Holbein.

Between 1923 and 1933 other suitable pictures were acquired, sometimes at sales at great houses and sometimes through dealers, who often acted as disinterested advisers as well when their personal enthusiasm for Parham and for the aims of its owners was aroused. The first to help them in this way was John Major of Vicars Bros., who later introduced them to John Quilter of Gooden & Fox. Quilter carried out endless research for them and became a close friend as well as nearly always acting for them at sales. When Clive died, one of the warmest personal tributes of all came in a letter from John Quilter to Veronica in which he said simply 'I learnt what is best in life from him. Of course your mother and he are really bracketed'. While to Alicia he wrote that 'Clive's kindness and encouragement were always wonderful, but from his quiet example and ideals grew my great admiration and affection.'

The first two sales at houses of comparable dates to Parham were at Quenby in Leicestershire in 1920, and in 1922 at Boston House near Brentford, on the western fringe of London. The former produced a portrait of the second Lord Darnley, an extraordinary figure who subsisted precariously on the Continent partly through his unusual (and presumably much needed) talent for conjuring tricks. Boston House yielded three more conventional portraits of the school of Van Somer which fitted in particularly well at Parham; a picture by James Seymour of the famous Arab thoroughbred Godolphin Barb, originally from the collection of the Dukes of Leeds; and two good portraits by Devis and Hogarth. Also in 1922 came the Burdett-Coutts sale, at which portraits by Gainsborough and from the school of Reynolds were bought to go with the other eighteenth-century pictures already acquired, as well as a fine profile portrait of David Garrick by Van Der Gucht.

The last major acquisitions before the influx from Paddockhurst in 1933 came from the Surrenden Dering sale in 1928. A Miss Mary Dering had married in 1672 an earlier Sir Thomas Knatchbull, another of Alicia's direct ancestors; and her sister Elizabeth was the great-grandmother of Harriet Anne Southwell, who married Sir Cecil Bysshopp, 12th Lord Zouche. These ramifications may seem a little far-flung to the average reader, but they were meat and drink to Alicia in her patient researches into the history of Parham, and her admirable concern to bring together under its roof anything connected with it that was worth preserving. The Dering family were therefore doubly at home at Parham, and no less than fourteen portraits of members of the family were bought at the sale, by Cornelis Johnson, Van Somer, Lely and Kneller, and a further Lely of Catharine of Braganza. But now the time had come to take a breather. A great many pictures had been acquired, nearly £30,000 had gone on capital expenditure on the house, chiefly on alterations to the east and west wings, and on water and electricity supplies, not forgetting £1,200 on a Wendy house and £3,100 on a swimming-pool for the children, which remains in excellent condition to this day. Clive was a very rich man, but at the end of 1930 even he thought it wise to retrench, in line with the rest of the society in which he moved, and when Veronica and Lavinia went to a boarding school, the house in Grosvenor Square was actually shut up for two years, and left in the hands of a caretaker. Britain came off the Gold Standard for the second time in 1931, and there was a widespread idea that the end of western civilisation was nigh. However, two years after the pictures from Paddockhurst had settled in at Parham, the old urge revived, and eleven pictures were bought in 1935. These included a superb Bellotto of Venice, measuring seven feet by four, which cost a mere £500, and Romney's portrait of Emma Hamilton as Ariadne, only 2ft.7ins by 2ft.2ins, but which at £2,835 was almost five times more expensive. Also acquired were two Zoffanys of Master and Miss Sylvester and a splendid picture by Reynolds of Omai, the chief of Otaheite who accompanied Captain Cook back to England on a visit from the South Seas. Later the Pearsons acquired a small needlework picture showing Omai being presented by Banks to Queen Charlotte and the four princesses. Lack of space prevents the inclusion here of full details of most of the portraits, but Omai is such an exotic and striking figure that he deserves exceptional treatment. He had taken refuge in Tahiti when the men of Borabora had captured his native island of Raiatea, and there he had met the crews of two ships in Captain Cook's expedition, *Dolphin* and *Endeavour*. He asked to be taken on board the *Adventure*, under Captain Furneaux, who obligingly recorded him as an able seaman, since stray passengers were against regulations. They set sail on 23 December 1773 and finally reached Spithead on 14 July 1774. Omai was immediately introduced into the highest circles, first to Lord Sandwich, First Lord of the Admiralty, who in turn presented him to the King at Kew. After being inoculated against smallpox, and taking some time to recover, Omai was entertained by Lord Sandwich at Hinchingbrooke where his method of cooking meat out of doors was so much liked that Banks wrote that 'he is desired to cook again today not out of curiosity but for the real desire of eating meat so dress'd . . . so much natural politeness I never saw in any man: wherever he goes he makes friends and has not I believe as yet a foe.' Omai later dined with Dr Johnson at the house of his friends the Thrales at Streatham, and with Fanny Burney and her family, and on no less than ten occasions with the Royal Philosophers' Club. He mastered chess and also backgammon, at which he beat Baretti at Streatham, and was taken by Banks to stay with Lord Mulgrave near Whitby in Yorkshire, where he alarmed the son of another guest by swimming with him on his back far out to sea. But all was well, and Omai was soon being entertained on the Admiralty yacht in which Lord Sandwich was inspecting the royal dockyards. His portrait remains very much at home at Parham.

A further group of eighteenth-century pictures was soon bought by Clive from the sale of the collection of Sir H. Hughes-Stanton, RA, including four small oval portraits, two by Zoffany and two by William Roth, and a scene from *The Beggar's Opera* by H. Singleton. In 1937 a further group with theatrical connections was acquired, consisting of five charming portraits of John Fawcett, the Manager of Covent Garden, and his wife and three sons by G. H. Harlow, a gifted artist who would certainly be better known had he not died at the age of thirty-one. Picture-buying was once again in full swing, and in the same year the Pearsons bought from Mrs Roper-Lumley-Holland two very desirable portraits by John Michael Wright, one of them of Lord Charles Somerset, which was eventually sold on to the Duke of Beaufort. Two more dispersals followed in 1938. Lord Feilding's sale produced the Infanta Maria Anna by Gonzalez and an early seventeenth-century Earl of Monmouth, as well as the admirable *Men o' War Becalmed*, a luminous work by Samuel Scott; while Lord Savile's sale at Rufford Abbey provided three characteristic Parham portraits of the sixteenth century, of Ambrose Earl of Warwick, his brother Lord Henry Dudley, and an anonymous physician, all high-class products of the English school.

It would be a mistake to think that the problems and stringencies of wartime would prevent the Pearsons from carrying on collecting. In 1942 they bought, for a total of less than £150, three small but highly relevant pictures for Parham at the sale of the Harington collection. These were the first Lord Harington, Queen Elizabeth's guardian during her childhood, and his daughter Lucy, and Charles I's sister Elizabeth, the Winter Queen of Bohemia. These were followed in 1943 by an admirable Gainsborough of Captain Charles Phipps, RN, with a faint Banks connection, and in 1945 a branch of the Seymour family at East Knoyle in Wiltshire sent some important Tudor portraits to Christie's, and Parham gained Edward VI and Henry Howard, Earl of Surrey, both by Guilim Stretes; Robert Devereux, Earl of Essex by Gheeraerdts; and Lord Henry Seymour by Zuccaro, for a total of £1,379. At this stage, when the collection might just possibly have been allowed to rest on its laurels, a fresh and genuine reason for adding to it suddenly arose. When Rupert Gunnis, the great connoisseur of English houses and sculpture, urged them to open Parham to the public in 1947, the Pearsons' first reaction was that it was not a show place: however much time and trouble and money they might have devoted to it, the public would simply not be interested. But on consideration they allowed themselves to be persuaded, partly by the enthusiasm of Rupert Gunnis and other connoisseurs, partly by the financial aspect, and partly because they came to feel a genuine urge to share what they had achieved at Parham with any visitors who might be interested. Their three daughters were all married, and although visiting grandchildren would later be greeted with open arms, Parham was meanwhile a very large house for the owners, now in their late fifties, to occupy on their own in the rigours of post-war austerity. Facilities for entertaining on the prewar scale, and even the inclination to do so, had both dwindled considerably. However, if the house was to be thrown open, it must be made as powerful an attraction as possible for the public, and this provided not just an excuse, but in their eyes a genuine and welcome reason for giving a further boost to the picture collection. The works which they now proceeded to buy form a third category in the overall collection.

Perhaps the greatest treasure to be acquired in this way was the equestrian portrait of Henry Frederick, Prince of Wales, the elder brother of Charles I, who died, full of promise and having inspired boundless expectations, at the age of eighteen in 1612. The artist is now confirmed as Robert Peake, and the illustration indicates, better than any words, the transformation brought about when the picture was cleaned before being lent to the Treasure Houses of Britain exhibition in Washington in 1985. At £6,500 it was, even in its uncleaned state, the most expensive picture the Pearsons had so far bought. With it came a portrait of James I by Van Somer, and the concentration of Tudor and Stuart portraits which thus came together in the Great Hall is almost unique outside the royal collections themselves. First there is Queen Elizabeth herself (though it must be admitted that doubts have been cast on her identity, which this is not the place to go into). There is her elder half-brother Edward VI; her early favourite, Robert Dudley Earl of Leicester, with his brothers Ambrose Earl of Warwick and Lord Henry Dudley; her later favourite Robert Devereux Earl of Essex; the most significant of all her advisers, William Cecil Lord Burghley; her successor James I; his Queen, Anne of Denmark, and their eldest son Prince Henry Frederick; and to round off the group, her little goddaughter whose son laid the foundation stone of Parham.

Other sixteenth- and seventeenth-century portraits acquired were Charles I as Prince of Wales by Mytens, and another picture of his sister the Winter Queen of Bohemia by Van Somer, and Sir Edward and Lady Bysshopp also by Mytens. On top of this, there was another crucial addition in store. By the time the house was opened, Lady Zouche was herself again moving to a smaller house, and offered to lend the Pearsons a further group of fine Parham portraits (eight Bysshopps, three Asshetons and one Grosvenor) and these were ultimately bought from her in 1964.

Mention must also be made of a fourth category of pictures which were now acquired. The Smileys had by now settled at Castle Fraser, and there was for a time a possibility that it might be opened to the public under their ownership rather than being handed over to the National Trust for Scotland as eventually happened. The idea was that, like Parham, it would have needed appropriate contents of high quality to attract visitors, and to this end the Pearsons began a collection of the later Stuarts which in the end fitted in happily with the earlier ones already at Parham, which in turn followed on from the original Tudor nucleus. They included the Old Pretender by F. de Troy, his brother Cardinal York by A. Longhi, his son Prince Charles Edward, the Young Pretender, followed by two more pictures by Largillière, one of the Old Pretender and another of Princess Louisa Maria Teresa Stuart. And in 1952 there was a sale at a house belonging to another branch of the Knatchbull family at Babington, in Somerset, which produced four more members of Alicia's forebears who fitted in very happily. Also acquired in 1952 were a good portrait of Charles II by Verelst, two of his mistresses, the Duchesses of Portsmouth and Cleveland by Lely, and his sister-in-law Anne Hyde, Duchess of York by the same artist. In the next year, 1953, there was a great sale at Sotheby's of the contents of Ashburnham Place, not far from Parham, which produced another Largillière of the Old Pretender, this time as a child; a portrait of Charles II's favourite sister Henriette, Duchess of Orleans ('Minette') by Mignard, and a Vandyke of Charles I which (whether it is by Vandyke or not) was already in the inventory at Ashburnham in 1679. Also bought afterwards were portraits of Charles Brandon Duke of Suffolk, who had boldly married Henry VIII's sister, and Mary of Modena, the second wife of James II, by Wissing.

The house now contained a magnificent collection; not a varied assortment of grand pictures of the kind bought by Lord Cowdray on the advice of Duveen, but primarily an integrated assembly of portraits all connected in some way with Parham and its history; and a selection of 'country-house' pictures discerningly chosen. The tempo of acquisition now slowed down, but the habit of collecting could not be broken, and the quality of what was bought was certainly sustained. In 1960 a portrait of a lady, conceivably Mary Tudor, by a close follower of Holbein, was bought for £10,000, and in 1965, a year after Clive's death, an irresistible group of Banks, his Swedish secretary Solander, and Omai, by William Parry, was added to the collection, along with a fine work by Claude Deruet, *The Triumph of Louis XIII and His Wife*, from the Spencer-Churchill collection at Northwick Park, whose owner's sister had married Clive's brother Harold. Also from the same source came a large and handsome lion, made of Coade stone, which was set into the wall of the old water tower. The final seal was set on the collection, very characteristically, by Alicia, when she bought Stubbs's remarkable picture of a kangaroo. The skin of this animal had been brought to England by Banks, and acting on his instructions Stubbs is said to have inflated the skin and painted from it the first European picture of the species.

Other minor pictures were bought from time to time, a few more were sold for various reasons, and others were given by the Pearsons to their daughters when they married and set up house. There was always something going on: catalogues to be scrutinised, pictures to be sent for, to see if they fitted in at Parham. When a picture arrived, excitement would run high, Clive would give the brief order 'Offer it up!' and two acolytes would hold it against the wall to see if it was acceptable for Parham. Sometimes their hopes were fulfilled, sometimes disappointed. But no butterfly collector would take more care to seek out a rare specimen than the Pearsons in their hunts for missing pieces in the historical mosaic that they had so lovingly built up.

This aspect of their lives was of such importance to them that it merits analysis that might otherwise have seemed excessive. But the trouble that they took to trace and examine possible acquisitions was also a great inspiration to their advisers, whose enthusiasm was also soon kindled and remained burning to the end. Equal trouble was taken about all kinds of other aspects of Parham, especially as regards the quality of work done and the importance of avoiding any discordant note; but it was only the pictures that had this direct historical association with the house, and however skilful the reconstruction and reorganisation of the actual fabric, it was the pictures that brought it back to life so effectively, in human terms, after its previous slow decline.

Far more important than the furniture, and at least equal in the Pearsons' eyes to the quest for relevant pictures, was the pursuit of antiquarian books. As with the pictures, there was an influx of books from Paddockhurst when the house was sold on Lady Cowdray's death in 1933, and they fell into two different categories in which Lord Cowdray had been interested, and of which exact details have survived. He had collected books rather in the same way as pictures, and Alicia and Clive gave him a particularly well-chosen Christmas present in 1918 in the shape of William Dugdale's *Imbanking and Drayning*, published in 1662. He had already amassed a wide range of books on natural history, starting with fifty-two volumes of *Curtis's Botanical Magazine*, covering the years 1787 to 1846, which he bought from Bumpus for £1 a copy. The second covered the whole spectrum of English literature and history, represented by the *Cambridge Modern History* and the *Cambridge History of English Literature*, each in fourteen volumes; the works of Fielding, Froude and Madame D'Arblay, and the eleven volumes of Lord Campbell's *Lives of the Lord Chancellors*. Eighteen folio volumes of the *Letters of Horace Walpole*, and of more recent date, no less than seven volumes of *The Boyhood of Edward VII*. There was also a six-volume catalogue of the Louvre and a fine folio of *Views* by Van Der Meulen, mostly of towns besieged or captured by Louis XIV, stamped on the cover with his arms. The royal stamp on French bindings does not indicate that it was in any sense the king's own copy or that it came from the royal library. It merely shows that the book is from a royal source, and may have been one of hundreds of copies presented by or on behalf of the king to an ambassador or to a holder of one of the infinite number of offices attached to the court and the government. In England, on the other hand, armorial stamps were used more sparingly, and genuinely indicate that the book concerned was the property of the holder of the arms, and that he had acquired it either by inheritance or because he wanted it. But this particular book, or possibly the twenty-three folio volumes of the *Cabinet du Roi* which had been acquired by Lord Cowdray in 1917 for £560, may well have been what set Alicia off on what was to become the most important area, strictly from the expert's point of view, of her collecting career. So knowledgeable was she to become in the field of armorial book-stamps that the leading antiquarian book dealers, several of whom became her valued friends, would sometimes seek her advice in identifying obscure coats of arms on bindings; and the collector Major J. R. Abbey, who lived only three miles from Parham, tried to persuade her to compose a reference book on the subject, the only existing one (by Davenant) being seriously defective. Her natural diffidence prevented her from undertaking it, and in any case she was probably far happier tracking down the books themselves. But the greater part of the catalogue of the library at Parham, which gives details of the title, author, date and size of the books, is written out in her own exceptionally clear hand, and often also gives the date and source of acquisition and sometimes, though not always, the price.

The armorial stamps include the arms of Louis XV (as well as XIV), Philip V of Spain (on the *Office for Holy Week*) and Anne of Austria (appropriately enough on *Regicide in England*). There is also Henry Frederick Prince of Wales's copy of Rondelet's *Histoire de Poissons* and George II's copy of the *Act to Punish Mutiny*, published in 1735, and a copy of Speed's *Theatre of Great Britain* (1611) with the arms of the Duke of Newcastle. Next comes William III's copy of the *Vindication of Robert III of Scotland* by Viscount Tarbat. All these were acquired by Alicia, but in January 1946 Clive took a hand himself and bought from Maggs, for no more than £60, one book stamped with the arms of Edward VI, two with those of Charles II and a fourth (West's *Simboleography*) with those of Charles I's sister Elizabeth, the Winter Queen. A number of others belonged to the Old Pretender, including Montfaucon's *Italian Diary*, and his younger son, Cardinal York (*Il Vangelo in Meditazioni*, 1792). Also acquired were the *Prediche del reve* by Savanorola (arms of Lord Herbert of Cherbury) and a bible and a prayer book of George III. Books with the arms of the subjects of portraits in the house were especially prized, and there were further historical and religious books which had belonged to most of the kings of England from James I to George III, with a particular accent on the Stuarts. The main emphasis throughout lay on the intrinsic interest of the owner, but the contents are often of general appeal as well.

The second area in which Alicia came to specialise was in books concerning all forms of natural history from the sixteenth to the nineteenth centuries. Obviously the quality of the printing and engraving, and the attractions of the colour plates, make these books far more accessible and attractive to the eye, and the collection at Parham, formed at a time when fine examples could be picked up by the systematic searcher for a very few pounds each, remains a delight. After her mother's death, Veronica took great trouble to put small selections from the library on special display in the Long Gallery. At various times between 1976 and 1982 these miniature exhibitions reflected the various categories of books in which Alicia had been particularly interested. The first display was of natural history books. The second, a group of sumptuously produced books connected in some way with George IV. Thirdly, the armorial book stamps already described, and fourthly, the delightful panoramic rolls, which are not books at all, but lengths of illustrated paper wound round a central core when not on view. Next came a selection of books on Mexico, especially its topography and natural history. Then a group which had been collected almost by accident, on the Great Exhibition of 1851, and a fine selection of books on the early explorers, leading off, in all directions in time and space, from the central figure of Sir Joseph Banks. Then came some of the books collected by Robert Curzon, Lord Zouche at Parham in the nineteenth century: some of these were acquired from Lady Zouche with the house, but others had been sold off over the years and were eagerly reacquired for Parham whenever Alicia's excellent network of dealers brought them to her attention. But she also always kept her own eyes open, and on one occasion spotted, on a pavement barrow, a copy of the *Memoirs of Petitot* (1828) stamped with the arms of William Wyndham, Lord Grenville, Chancellor of the University of Oxford. She bought it for sixpence. The last display put on by Veronica was of plates in French illustrated books, chiefly architectural and topographical, many of which had come from Paddockhurst, though in this field, as elsewhere, Alicia had always been at pains to build on existing foundations and to add worthwhile examples to an existing nucleus. It is hardly surprising that when Mr Dring of Quaritch wrote a letter of condolence on Alicia's death, Veronica was able to reply that 'some of my mother's happiest hours were spent at Quaritch'.

Curiously enough, the five years between 1944 and 1948 were those in which Alicia acquired most books: annual totals of 141, 249, 313, 416 and 100 were added to the library, the figure for 1947 including 77 bought from a dispersal of books by her nephew Lord Brabourne. Earlier, it was only in three years in the 1930s that more than twenty antiquarian books had been bought, the year 1933 in which the South Library was created being an obvious turning-point, which itself arose largely as a result of a carefully selected choice of the books at Paddockhurst, many of the rest being sold, along with other miscellaneous contents, at an auction at the house. But the habit of collecting dies hard, if at all, if you live in a big house, and over thirty books were acquired in each of the next four years. Later, a professional cataloguer came to work at Parham but was apparently not instructed to record all the details that had been set down by Alicia in earlier years.

7
Aircraft Companies and BOAC

The sale of Mexican Eagle to Shell in 1920 had given Lord Cowdray and Clive the opportunity to invest the proceeds in a wide range of new ventures: electricity in Chile and later in England, Spain and Greece; the search for oil all over the world; and the participation in Lazards. These were the chief projects in the 1920s, though there were other smaller ones as well. Now, with the well-timed sale of the control of most of the Pearson interests in North and South America in 1928, the year before the Wall Street crash, new opportunities had once more to be considered.

As before, new technology and the prospect of supplying the new needs of modern times were what appealed to Clive. Now it was air travel, still a little-known and rather glamorous novelty, an uncertain but not an expensive one for the consumer. (In 1934 the fare from London to Jersey was £5 return, or £4 from Exeter or Brighton.) Small, optimistic companies sprang up like mushrooms, often run by carefree officers from the Royal Flying Corps who having survived the perils of the war were quite ready to embark on equally hazardous commercial ventures. They had no commercial air experience, but then nor had anyone else. Clive, however, unlike most of his rivals, was able to apply the methods which had made Pearson's such a triumphantly successful group for nearly half a century: conscientious attention to detail, patience, a curious mixture of brusqueness and consideration and generosity in their treatment of employees, and a habit of regarding hard work as indispensable at all levels, but with the chief example set from the top. The aircraft companies were not to be the great money-spinners that the contracting and oil companies had been, but they were not losers either, and they were making good headway in unfamiliar territory when their nature was changed by the coming of war in 1939.

The first company to be invested in was Simmonds Aircraft Ltd, which had been incorporated in the ill-chosen year of 1928, and had become insolvent by August 1929, by which time it had made and sold thirty aircraft and had orders for another 160 spread over the next three years.

Captain Harold Balfour MP had flown the planes and approved of them. Balfour, who was to play a considerable part in this story over the next ten years, had joined the Royal Flying Corps from the Army and had twice been decorated in the First World War. He had entered Parliament in 1929, and had specialised in aviation matters to the extent of being invited in April 1935 to join the board of what was at that stage called United Airways. He became Parliamentary Under-Secretary for Air in 1938. Although he and Clive were of different temperaments, and never became friends like Runciman and Leo d'Erlanger, Balfour was very much a figure to be reckoned with, particularly when the time came for government subsidies for civil airlines, and for the later headaches brought on by BOAC.

Whitehall Securities invested £45,000 in Simmonds Aircraft, renamed it Spartan Aircraft and moved its operations to Cowes. At the end of 1930 they also acquired, for £89,000, a 50% stake in Saunders Roe, the leading manufacturers of flying-boats and other aircraft, and Clive recruited Sir Arthur Gouge from Short Bros. to propel the company forward. Then in March 1934 a proposal was received from the Great Western Railway, the Southern Railway and Railway Air Services, that Spartan Airlines should operate a Channel Islands service, and although nothing came of this at first, Whitehall Securities also acquired an interest in Jersey and Guernsey Airways, finally buying out the original owner in 1939. The weak points of the existing service were 'thoroughly bad organisation in Jersey; a timetable that varied with the tides; the risk of planes landing in the sea with engine trouble; and the absence of wireless'. Fresh finance and competent administration were all that was required to improve matters, and in the next year six D.H. 86 planes, capable of cruising at 155 m.p.h., operated the service from Croydon to Guernsey. The flight took one and a half hours including a stop at Bournemouth. Needless to say, with his invariably keen interest in technical matters, Clive often went up in these planes himself, carefully concealing the fact that he was a nervous passenger, although Veronica remembers seeing his white knuckles gripping the seat in front of him.

He incidentally became a director of the Southern Railway in 1936, but no details have survived about the part he played in their affairs, which was probably restricted to attendance at monthly board meetings, and the odd shrewd comment when consulted. When travelling, he concealed his metal director's pass in a leather holder, and would only show it in a thoroughly furtive fashion to the ticket collectors – a good example of the way in which he recoiled naturally from anything approaching ostentatious behaviour. The Southern Railway, unlike the others, was actually taken over by the Government in 1939 so that they would have direct control over it as part of their general direction of the war effort. This again would have reduced the part that Clive played as an ordinary director. But his personal interest in trains was keen, and is also reflected in the books on the subject that he began to collect after the war; it went back to the importance to Pearson's of the Tehuantepec Railway in Mexico, and all the advantages that had their origins in it. Later he set up a splendid model railway in the Long Gallery at Parham, and on one occasion he was playing trains there with Veronica when Harold Balfour arrived on a business visit of some consequence. Cridland escorted him up to the Long Gallery on the top floor, but they both had to wait at the door – in some impatience in the case of Balfour – until Clive, quite unperturbed, had finished giving Veronica her demonstration, and was ready to give Balfour his attention. (Arranging journeys for the children was also a source of pleasure to him. One summer they were all sent up by sea to Aberdeen for the holiday at Castle Fraser, and in 1935 he sent Veronica and Lavinia by train from San Antonio in Texas to Los Angeles and Hollywood and from there back to New York, a journey of four nights and three days which they enjoyed hugely.)

In September 1935 came the formation of British Airways, incorporating the existing aircraft companies owned by Whitehall Securities, grouped under United Airways, with another company called Hillman Airways, controlled by Erlangers. Erlangers and Whitehall Securities had now each invested £226,000 in the group. It was an entirely suitable marriage: Hillman Airways ran services first to Ramsgate and Clacton, then to Paris and Vichy, and later to Glasgow, Liverpool and Belfast. The United Airways side of the company worked routes from London to Blackpool, Morecambe, Carlisle and the Isle of Man, besides those already mentioned. Five months later, in February 1936, British Airways extended its activities by signing a three-year contract for a mail and passenger service to Malmö in Sweden, via Copenhagen, with a subsidy of £25,000 a year from the Government. The seeds had been sown for the provision of a great public service, to which public funds were to make an ever-increasing contribution. A night mail and freight service to Hanover was begun in May, and in the following March an experimental service was embarked on to West Africa. Plans were also made for a passenger and mail service to Buenos Aires, though this never went into operation. Meanwhile yet another company, British Continental Airways, was acquired in 1936. It already ran flights to Belgium and Holland, but trouble arose following a crash in which its chief pilot and the first officer on the plane were killed. There were serious criticisms of British Airways' ground organisation and equipment for night flying in the press and in the House of Commons, arising partly from a genuine watchdog feeling of protecting the public, and partly no doubt from envious commercial rivalry against those who had got in on the ground floor. British Continental was not actually amalgamated with British Airways until August 1937, when the base was moved from Gatwick to Heston. The service to Cologne and Hanover was extended to Berlin, and the Prime Minister Neville Chamberlain flew to Munich in a British Airways plane in September 1938. The photograph of him on the steps of the aeroplane is one of the best known in recent history, and the advertisement value of the words 'British Airways' on the steps must have been considerable.

Perhaps not surprisingly, not all went smoothly in this series of amalgamations. Clive expected to find the same level of business standards from new associates as those he kept himself, and was never one to tone down what he thought of people who did not live up to them. A memorandum survives in which he wrote of another air company:

They are arrogant and insulting. They show inexperience in affairs and are weak and small. They find themselves in a business which instead of producing early profits needs building up, is competitive and burdensome. They show no patience or courage but seek to blame British Airways. They are merely kidding themselves when they say they have the public and general good in mind.

They are cunning. They lie in wait and torpedo us apparently from spite, when opportunity offers, and obstruct at the moment when we are to sign the contract . . .

There was no doubt another side to the story, but this passage gives a good example of Clive's powers of analysis, his clarity of thought and his verbal punch when roused.

Plans were now made to extend the service still further, with flights to Warsaw via Berlin, and Budapest via Frankfurt, with further Government subsidies of £19,500 for the Brussels service and £53,000 for Warsaw and Budapest, to cover the period between May and September 1939. Scottish Airways, which ran flights from Glasgow to Campbelltown and Islay, and Highland Airways, which served Aberdeen, Inverness, Orkney and Shetland, were also brought into the fold in May.

The Pearson companies all round had made such splendid recovery since the horrors of 1930 and 1931 that the senior management all received a recovery bonus in 1937, Mr J. H. Macdonald receiving no less than £50,000 over two years, and the others, who had successfully borne the heat of the day, were rewarded with smaller but still substantial sums.

To give an idea of the financial position of the aircraft companies themselves, British Airways estimated for a surplus of nearly £16,000 on the Stockholm route and £18,000 on Berlin for 1937/8, but a loss of £6,000 on Paris, where there was no doubt greater competition, and of £2,600 on the instructional school. This left a surplus of £25,500 on these routes, against which had to be set a cost of £40,000 for the running costs of the London terminal, with its own administration and advertising costs. The overall deficit was therefore to be in the region of £14,000. The more ambitious plans for 1938/9 would mean a deficit of £137,000, but by using the reserve for contingencies, and excluding interest on capital, the shortfall could be reduced, on paper, to just over £12,000. By this time British Airways employed 290 men and 35 women.

In November 1938 Clive was informed by Sir Kingsley Wood, the Secretary of State for Air, of 'tentative plans to establish a public body to take over both British Airways and Imperial Airways'. Clive's first reaction was to lay plans for protecting the interests of shareholders, since both companies had incurred heavy expenses in building up services which were already becoming profitable, and British Airways' Paris service already brought in revenue of £70,000 a year. At a meeting with the Permanent Under-Secretary and his first deputy on 8 December Clive insisted that if the Government wanted to take over the company 'which was in a position to do important work and which was of considerable utility, it was only fair that the cost of *producing* should be recognised as the takeover price'.

In March of that year the Cadnam Report had criticised Imperial Airways for various shortcomings and most seriously for having declared an increased dividend of 9% when in receipt of a Government subsidy. In the summer the Secretary of State decided to inspect the British Airways base at Heston and summoned Clive, who was on holiday in the Isle of Wight, to show him round. Unfortunately, however Clive was prevented by fog from flying to join him, and Alan Campbell Orde, the Director of Operations, had to take his place without warning. The Minister's PPS handed him a note from Sir John Reith stating briefly that the Government had decided to put the two organisations together to form a

RACKHAM RECTORY,

~~May 1940.~~

INVASION

1. If Germans actually reach this area, we are to "stay put", and not to go into the roads which will be used by the Military alone.

2. If you have urgent reason for going out for anything, only paths and fields may be used.

3. It is most important that each household should make sure of having in hand some seven days' supply of food. Always keep a stock of Flour especially (and Baking Powder), for Bread will be difficult to obtain. DO THIS NOW.

4. When the Home Guard are ordered to their Stations, which means actual invasion, you should go to your Food Centre (Parham House) and take with you,
    (a) The outer cover at least of your Ration Book.
    (b) Bags and baskets for carrying the tins, etc.
    (c) Money.

    The food allotted for each person costs 6/- It consists of -
    $3\tfrac{3}{4}$ lbs. biscuits)
    1 tin corned beef)
    1 tin soup)
    1 tin condensed milk)   = 6s. 0d.
    1 lb. sugar)
    4 ozs. margarine)
    2 ozs. tea)

5. Although this supply is to be fetched by you as soon as invasion really occurs, it is not to be used until your other food has been finished. You <u>may not</u> need it at all in which case you should keep it most carefully and return it to the Food Officer.

6. There ought to be plenty of Milk, but you may have to fetch it yourself.

7. Apply to the Rectory at Rackham if you are uncertain what to do.

    H. W. Weatherhead, Voluntary Food Officer.

    Veronica Rueff, Deputy Voluntary Food Officer.

Invasion advice, May 1940, signed by Veronica as Deputy Voluntary Food Officer.

Alicia, Miranda Smiley, Hugh Gibson and Dione, Parham 1949.

Mrs Cecil Heywood, the Queen of Sweden and Alicia, Parham, 1957.

Clive with Andy Smiley, 1955.

Clive's car in Fountain Court, Parham, 1958.

Miranda Smiley's coming-out dance at Parham, June 1958. Lavinia and Miranda in the Great Parlour.

Rupert Gunnis and Angela Campbell-Preston at Blair Castle, April 1958.

Alicia and Clive at Parham.

There was a young fellow called Brown
Who called on a Lady in Town,
  He entered her Bower
  And proffered a Flower
But she said "Both your Stockings are down"

26. FROM LORENZO DE' MEDICI'S LA NENCIA DA BARBERINO, S.A.

From Paul Kristeller's Early Florentine Woodcuts, *in the library at Parham, annotated by Alicia.*

Paddy Tritton, Veronica's second husband, at Gosport, 1964.

Clive in the 'Sprite', with Alicia: by the swimming pool at Parham, July 1964.

Alicia and Clive outside Parham.

public corporation on the lines of the BBC (completely ignoring the very different natures of the two concerns). The unfortunate Campbell Orde was so appalled by the prospect that he was unable to eat the lunch at which he had to act as host, and was also disappointed to find that the Minister appeared to know little or nothing about the business in hand. Both Whitehall Securities and Erlangers bank did their utmost to resist the move, but of course in vain. (In the 1980s the truth that both travellers and also crews of long- and short-distance trips require entirely different treatment was finally recognised. Small was once again identified as beautiful and local short distance airlines began to be founded and to flourish.)

Five months later, when BOAC was actually formed, a leader of formidable talents was appointed as director-general in the shape of Leslie Runciman. He had already accepted the position of chief executive and vice-chairman on the appointment of Lord Reith as chairman, but Reith was soon to become disenchanted with BOAC, and later expected a post in the Government, probably as Secretary of State for Air. He reluctantly stayed on as chairman (a post he had previously held for a few months at Imperial Airways) partly in response to a letter from Clive saying that it was 'outstandingly desirable that you should be chairman of the corporation, and I greatly hope you will have no hesitations'. Whatever Reith's foibles (and they later led to his being quite unable to get on with Churchill) Clive recognised the value of having a powerful man in the chair, and moreover one who knew his way round Whitehall.

Runciman, on the other hand, was a shining example of the ideal results of a classical education: his precision of mind and vigour of expression were at least the equal of Clive's, and he had the additional advantage of fifteen years' practical commercial experience in his own family shipping company in Newcastle, and more important still, of much first-hand flying experience, which included the formation and command of 607 Squadron, a territorial air force unit based in County Durham. His father had been President of the Board of Trade in Asquith's Government, and he and Clive made a formidable pair. Perhaps it was a greater independence of mind that led him later to describe Clive as 'an obedient man' – not an aspect of his character that would often strike others. But he may perhaps have been referring to Clive's willingness to seek expert advice in fields where he lacked direct experience, and then to follow it in what appeared to Runciman to be an unquestioning fashion. In fact, the reason why this had become a part of Clive's natural approach was simply that he had grown accustomed to assessing and taking over new projects that were far too numerous and diverse for one man to have direct experience of them. Runciman, on the other hand, was a real expert on aeroplanes and knew himself, or certainly thought he knew, the answers to most of the questions that arose. He was also thirteen years younger than Clive, and perhaps closer to the height of his powers. Hitherto, Clive had had little to do with larger-than-life characters, with the exception of his own father, and both Reith and Runciman, in their different ways, must have been a stimulating contrast to the more run-of-the-mill businessmen with whom he had been dealing for many years. Yet the frustrations and more or less insoluble problems of civil aviation in wartime were later to outweigh the pleasure to be gained from their company. Just after becoming vice-chairman Clive was interviewed by Nigel Tangye for the magazine *Aeronautics*, and was described as follows:

In his office he holds you at a distance, and nothing whatever will give away what he is thinking. But though in his office he may be somewhat awe-inspiring, away from it he is the most human of individuals. If you have three grown-up attractive daughters in these days, you can hardly avoid being frequently reminded of your mortal weaknesses . . . he likes the younger generation.

This may not be a profound analysis, but as a brief first-hand impression it is convincing. When he was surrounded by his wife and daughters, and a certain amount of noise arose, he would tell one of them patiently 'Just lower your voice to a loud scream'.

The first few months of the war were the lull before the storm. Clive had the misfortune to break his nose in an accident in a London taxi on Christmas Day. Runciman was appointed director-general at the end of January 1940, and Clive became part-time chairman on the departure of Reith in March. All BOAC's planes were henceforth at the disposal of the Air Ministry, and it is easy to understand that the civil side of aviation became the poor relation of the RAF when the Battle of Britain began in May, and the crisis of national survival began. In addition, BOAC was still suffering from teething troubles following its amalgamation of British and Imperial Airways in the previous summer, at a time when everybody concerned had plenty of other worries on their minds. Runciman expressed his view with customary lucidity and vigour in a report to Reith which sums up the internal problems of the Corporation long before it came to be trampled on by the RAF and the Ministry of Aircraft Production as well:

The two staffs were flung together on the outbreak of war. Imperial was by far the larger company, but had bitten off more than it could chew under the Empire Mail Scheme. Their attitude was one of high-handed secretiveness with the Air Ministry and with any others who sought to criticise them. Their training policy is short-sighted. The record of British Airways is incomparably better. Imperial had been a pioneer and seemed unable to forget it . . . Criticism is taken as disloyalty and the regime turns a blind eye to the standards of other countries.

It is on record that Clive's consistently meticulous requirements were considered pernickety and were a source of irritation to the former directors of Imperial Airways: for example, he would devote a long time to the subject of the width of margins in the typed minutes of board meetings, at a time when others considered that there were more important matters to be settled. On the other hand, Runciman commented on another occasion that British Airways were

small, inexperienced in the operation of long routes, and some of its staff too inclined to feel that the future belonged to them. Two such companies could not be easy bedfellows. There are still signs of jealousy, complacency, self-righteousness and even downright incompetence, but a start has been made, foundations laid and a structure is beginning to rise upon them.

Soon afterwards he stressed to Clive in a letter 'the vital importance of maintaining the main Empire routes. If our services on them break down, the effect on public opinion, especially East and South of Suez will be disastrous . . . and will almost certainly be taken as a sign that we were losing the war.' Meanwhile, Clive and Runciman, like many others accustomed to exercising authority, found themselves constantly restricted and hampered, often by people whom they regarded with some justification as their inferiors.

As early as 14 September 1939 an ominous meeting was held, at which Clive and Reith and Balfour were joined by Runciman. Reith described it in his autobiography as 'wholly unsatisfactory'. Balfour had made it clear that civil aviation in wartime was to be entirely subservient to the needs of the RAF; no new types of aircraft would be made, and in the words of the official history of BOAC, 'current types would have to die when cannibalisation yielded no more spares'. Balfour did however agree that no civil aircraft should be requisitioned without the Air Minister's consent, a form of protection which was not extended to BOAC personnel.

Balfour also did another good turn to BOAC, at some risk to himself. In the summer of 1940 he flew to America and bought three Boeing 314A flying-boats from Pan-American Airlines at a cost of £249,250 each. They were later of great value in moving supplies between Britain and West Africa, and were alone capable of providing transatlantic flights for VIPs. Although he was Under-Secretary of State, he did not possess the requisite authority for this deal, and according to A. J. P. Taylor's biography of Beaverbrook, when Balfour returned to London Beaverbrook refused to see him, Kingsley Wood, who was by then Chancellor of the Exchequer, rebuked him and Churchill himself wrote 'I really do not see how Government could be carried on if such unauthorised commitments were to be countenanced.' However, all was forgiven two years later when Churchill and Beaverbrook returned from Bermuda in one of the flying-boats, and the journey took several days less than it would have by warship, as had been originally planned.

On the important question of air safety, Runciman was writing to Clive as early as March 1940: 'We should seriously consider writing to the Air Ministry formally disclaiming responsibility for accidents on land routes to Egypt and India. We are unable to secure adequate supplies of life saving gear, because of RAF demands.' On 1 April the Secretary of State for Air required BOAC 'to place the whole of its undertaking at his disposal'. The Corporation was reminded that its role was 'to operate Air Transport services', and that anything else, including the training of pilots and the maintenance of planes, should be secondary. Yet, quite soon, there were to be contradictions and uncertainties. The Ministry of Aircraft Production, under Beaverbrook, would ask BOAC to undertake engine overhaul work, under contract, and many other important and complex tasks later arose which were outside the Corporation's original brief. For example, when Air Transport Auxiliary was formed under Gerard d'Erlanger, to recruit pilots to deliver fighters and bombers from the manufacturers to the squadrons, there was for some time doubt whether it was to be under the Minister or the Corporation. Staffing in general was to be a continuing problem. When the least useful members were disposed of or made redundant as time went by, they naturally felt aggrieved. On the other hand, the better they were the more likely they were to be appropriated by the Ministry of Aircraft Production.

However, in spite of all these difficulties, by December 1940 BOAC was running services to North America, Stockholm, West Africa, Egypt, South Africa, India and Australia, and three days before Christmas the

Secretary of State (Sir Archibald Sinclair) made a point of expressing to Clive his 'deep appreciation of all that the Corporation has achieved since the war began'. Early in the new year, however, Beaverbrook was writing to the Secretary of State:

For five months we have been trying to enlist the cooperation of BOAC on the provision of personnel for the Transatlantic Ferry Service Pool . . . on four separate occasions requests for the loan of BOAC personnel have been refused . . . Will you please persuade BOAC now to give us cooperation to the fullest extent, to yield us all the personnel asked for, and to make available to us all the resources we need. This would enable us to carry out a task that is of immense importance to us all.

Runciman's splendid comment on this letter was that 'its general tone seems to be rather that in which the Reichsprotector of Bohemia might write to Dr Benes complaining about the non-cooperation of the Czechs'. But on 8 March a detailed plan was produced for operating a regular Atlantic service, which was becoming of increasing importance with the stepping-up of various attempts to secure American help and cooperation of many kinds, of vital importance to the war effort.

Three days later Clive had an interview with Beaverbrook which he afterwards described as 'wholly unsatisfactory'. Beaverbrook had said categorically that he 'disapproved of civil aviation in wartime. The Australian service should be reduced or abolished.' Clive pointed out that 'our services were not civil but for mail and for the serving forces in the East'. He added that 'although quite unsympathetic, he was not rude, and he told me on leaving that he had been a friend of my father's and they often had lunch together.' Next day Beaverbrook wrote: 'We will be very glad to avail ourselves of the services of BOAC. But it would be necessary to place that portion of your organisation dealing with Atlantic flights under the control of this Ministry. Divided authority would be disastrous.' And three weeks later, 'I send you my very warm thanks for your helpful attitude' in the matter of flights to and from Canada. The Air Ministry agreed in May that BOAC should run the transatlantic flights, and Averell Harriman at the American Embassy confirmed that three US aircraft, capable of carrying a total of forty-seven passengers, would be made available to the Air Ministry for transporting 'Government officers of both nations only' across the Atlantic.

After June 1941 the picture changes again, with the allied forces in various parts of Africa, and in Syria, Palestine and Iraq needing more air transport. BOAC provided this from their headquarters in Cairo. They were also provided with three DC3 planes for a service from England to Lisbon, a vital neutral airport. The details of arranging these services would be tedious to relate, but a memorandum from Leo d'Erlanger as early as March of that year reveals that even civil aviation was acquiring a mystique of sorts, though not of course on the scale of the glamour of the fighter squadrons of the RAF. 'The Air carries with it', he wrote, 'a subtle though inspiring ideal . . . and many members of the various Air Forces are wishing for a post-war career in aviation.' Bombers would be easily convertible into passenger planes, and civil aviation was likely to be backed by 'ample public and if necessary private finance', especially in its Empire division.

By contrast with internecine strife which was so troublesome in London, there was also fruitful cooperation between BOAC and the RAF throughout the war. When Leslie Kemp, the managing director of Pearson's in Athens, had to leave Greece when the Germans arrived, Clive arranged for him to become Assistant to Robert Maxwell, the Middle East Regional Director of BOAC, in the execution of the Tedder Plan under which the first fourteen US Lease-Lend planes reached the Middle East. Clive's interest in the plan continued till the end of the war, and in 1952 Maxwell joined Kemp in Athens as his principal assistant.

Clive was still firmly in touch with his predecessor Reith, though the latter was constantly on the move, first as Minister of Transport from May to October 1940, next as Minister of Works until February 1942, and finally as Director of the Combined Operations Materials Department until the end of the war. In October 1941 Clive asked Reith to address the Minister of State on the necessity for machinery to bring together different parts of the Commonwealth in post-war civil aviation. BOAC had by now lost large numbers of skilled personnel to the RAF as well as to the Ministry of Aircraft Production, all of which added to Clive's already considerable dissatisfaction with his job. Having been used to running the family group of companies himself, with the unhampered support of his various lieutenants, it was supremely difficult for him, especially given his own formidable capacity for management, to come to terms with the constant interference of other government departments, which were in theory parallel to BOAC, but which in practice frequently barged in on its activities. He was also out of action again in the spring, when he wrote a very characteristic note, putting off an engagement saying 'I must now keep a long-deferred appointment to have my nose re-broken.'

Meanwhile the pattern of war operations was changing radically, with long-term plans being formed for the invasion of Italy which finally took place eighteen months later. These plans were of course known only to a handful at the top, and the fact that even someone as senior as Clive was inevitably kept in the dark led to further frustration. In April 1942 there was a new demand from the Air Ministry for BOAC to provide a service to Malta. Clive was most reluctant to agree to this, owing to shortages of technical and administrative staff, and the consequent risk of loss of efficiency and even of mechanical breakdowns. Balfour brushed these objections aside, but BOAC felt that it was being asked to lower its standards unacceptably, with its pilots being placed in danger of losing their licences, if not their lives.

All this was to go from bad to worse, and in June Runciman asked his Deputy in exasperation: 'Is the corporation doing essential work or is it not? If not we should greatly prefer to enlist as private soldiers in the Pioneer Corps. The Air Ministry should tell the Ministry of Labour to prevent our staff being transferred, sometimes even to civilian work.' Other senior members of his staff fell out with Runciman, including Major Ronald McCrindle, a former managing director of British Airways, who had primarily been legal adviser to Hillman Airways, where he had impressed Clive very favourably, and S. A. Sidmore, of Imperial Airways. In a letter which led to his departure from the corporation, the latter regretted that instead of becoming a 'real unit of the British Commonwealth' it was now widely regarded as 'an appendage of Whitehall Securities'. Whether there was in fact any justification for this perception, it was somewhat ironic in view of Clive's extreme reluctance to take on the job of chairman in the first place.

Clive had indeed brought in a number of trusted Pearson employees to improve the quality of his BOAC staff which no doubt included some mediocre elements. A good example has been recorded of the two types. After a troublesome meeting in Bristol, two former Imperial Airways employees were travelling in a taxi with one of Clive's faithful assistants who had worked for Pearson's for many years in Mexico. One of the trouble-makers said grumpily that in his opinion Clive Pearson was mad, whereupon the old hand from Mexico stopped the taxi, got out, and refused to attend any further BOAC meetings in Bristol again.

Things were now coming to a head. Runciman summed up the underlying uncertainty as follows: 'Should we regard ourselves as a branch of the Air Ministry, which means, as we see it, that we are debarred from making as a Corporation any public contribution to the discussion of air transport policy? Or should we regard ourselves as a body under the Act free to formulate policy and express it?' Clive now wrote to the Secretary of State in February 1943, ending his letter with Runciman's question verbatim, and leading up to it with a number of well-expressed contributory points: 'Not being an independent concern, we have not the discretion in directing policy such as would rest with a commercial undertaking; and not being a branch of the public service, we have not the defined and regulated authority of a service of the crown.' He recommended that the Board be strengthened and that the chairman should be one 'who at least informally would have access to the Ministers of the many Government departments with which the activities of the Corporation are concerned'. He complained of 'delay and wasted effort since the department of civil aviation is obliged to intervene between the Corporation and those with whom we need to be in direct contact about aircraft, airfields, spares and many other matters'. And on the question of post-war planning, which he believed 'can be done without detriment to the prosecution of the war', 'can we be informed whether it is intended that the Corporation should remain the sole British instrument for overseas air transport, or, if not, what limitations are intended?' Another member of the BOAC board, I. C. Geddes, drafted a more trenchant letter to the Secretary of State, saying that although it was right that the Corporation 'is entirely at your command',

control is being exercised today in a way which has forced us to believe it to be the wish of your Ministry not only to issue general instructions but substantially to usurp the functions of management, and so to place the Members of the Corporation in a position where, though they remain responsible for the management of the Corporation, they are unable to control its destinies. That is a situation which we are not prepared to accept.

Further dissatisfaction was expressed to Runciman by Alan Campbell Orde, Director of Operations at BOAC, and formerly Operations Manager at British Airways. He complained that the regional system for controlling operations no longer worked, and that there were difficulties involved in his being answerable both to Runciman and to his Deputy Director General, especially, no doubt, during Runciman's long absences abroad. There was also trouble from a Labour MP, Alfred Edwards, who criticised the fact that Clive was a director of the Southern Railway and another director, Geddes, was a director of the Orient Steam Navigation

Company, both of which might be in competition with BOAC in matters of freight transport after the war, or even sooner. Clive wearily pointed out to him that these directorships had been known to the Ministry when he and Runciman had been appointed, and that there would be room for all three forms of transport after the war. The cumulative effect of all these troubles must already have been severe, but the last straw then arose on the formation of Air Transport Command, to operate alongside Bomber and Fighter Commands. The need for this new creation had arisen from the great number of new transport squadrons being formed, with the help of the Americans, for the ultimate purpose of the allied landings in Sicily, Italy and Normandy. It was only natural that this extension needed to be run by the Air Ministry itself through Air Transport Command and not via BOAC and this factor came on top of the existing conflict, of priorities at the very least, between those whose task it was to win the war and those who were working primarily on planning civil aviation, on a Commonwealth scale, for the future.

Clive asked that BOAC should be brought further into the confidence of the Air Ministry. The Secretary of State, Sir Archibald Sinclair, replied in an interview with Clive that the method of strengthening the Board of BOAC, as Clive had asked, depended on decisions yet to be taken in conjunction with the Dominions, and asked Clive if he wanted to retire. The files that Clive preserved give the impression that his heart was no longer in the various problems that had accumulated, most of them insoluble as a result of changed circumstances. He had only taken on the job, which according to Runciman he hated, because he considered it his duty as war work, and perhaps also because in the back of his mind lay the memory that he had, through absolutely no fault of his own, not seen active service in the previous war, when his brother Geoffrey had been killed. (Apart from all his desk work throughout the Second World War, he was an assiduous fire-watcher on the rooftops of London during the blitz, and the present Lord Cowdray, who lost an arm on active service in 1940, remembers that his uncle would always take his heavy briefcase and carry it for him on long walks home after office hours in the blackout.) Yet in spite of all the frustrations, a cordial spirit somehow survived between Clive and his opposite numbers, and on one occasion Air Chief Marshal Sir Frederick Bowhill wrote to Clive after an unsatisfactory meeting: 'It was great fun, it may seem a funny expression to use, working with BOAC on the North Atlantic, because they were so keen and efficient.'

But the end had come. Clive wrote to Sinclair on 19 March that we feel our position has become unreal and our usefulness therefore limited: it would be more satisfactory to all concerned for this to be freely admitted by the present members tendering their resignation which they propose to do formally so soon as you are ready to appoint new members. Runciman will, if desired, carry on as Chief Executive in an honorary capacity until there is someone to take over his duties.

The Secretary of State was of course in a position to take a far wider view of the war than was available to the directors of BOAC. In his reply to Clive he pointed out the likely need in future to divert transport to military roles such as the dropping of parachute troops, the conveyance of other airborne forces, towing of gliders and participating in military operations generally, tasks that had never remotely been part of BOAC's role, but which were of course covered by the Air Ministry's takeover of BOAC in April 1940.

Besides Clive and Runciman, two of the other three members of the board resigned, Harold Brown and Irvine Geddes. The third, Gerard d'Erlanger, who was already running Air Transport Auxiliary, stayed on. In formally confirming the resignations to Sinclair, Clive felt able to thank him for his 'consideration and courtesy' and to express 'very true regret that we are unable to overcome our difference of opinion'. The fact is that neither side was in the wrong, but the parting of the ways was inevitable. Two Government White Papers were published containing the exchanges of letters, eight in all, between Clive and Sinclair and Balfour, the Under-Secretary. To illustrate the support that was felt at a high level for those who had resigned, one has only to read in *Hansard* (See Appendix B) the speeches made by Lord Rothermere and Lord Reith at the subsequent debate in the House of Lords on 14 April 1943, together with the very lame reply made for the Government by Lord Sherwood. They are an informed comment on the contribution made to the war effort, and to the plans for peacetime aviation made by Clive and his board. Lord Reith's speech, in addition, throws more light – admittedly from a subjective angle – on the obstacles and frustrations that had bedevilled Clive's life for the past three years.

8
The War at Home

When war broke out, one of the things that soon became clear was that life could not go on as before in a large house in London, and that unpredictable changes of many kinds were in the air. Servants would be called up for war work, and blackout, rationing, and all sorts of restrictions would be imposed. Clive's first reaction was to consider selling 32 Grosvenor Square, his London home for the past twenty years. The agents that he consulted advised that it would be quite useless to attempt to do so in November 1939, and the best plan would be to try to let it unfurnished for either five or seven years, after which the remaining fifty years of the lease from the Grosvenor Estate would be worth £14,000 or £15,000. They advised asking a rent of £1,000 a year inclusive of rates and taxes. It was offered to the Italian Delegation in London, but without result. The agents also quoted a price of £20,000 for anyone wishing to buy the whole lease. Meanwhile a caretaker was installed, and the RAF were allowed to keep a balloon in the front hall for use in the anti-aircraft barrage.

Clive moved at first into a suite in Grosvenor House nearby. But he was intolerably disturbed by the noise of the band in the evenings, and transferred first to the Ritz, which was quieter and also rather nearer to Parliament Street, and then to a series of rented flats where members of the family could occasionally join him when they were free from their duties. He was, however, constantly on the move during the first half of the war, commuting on BOAC business between London, Bristol and Parham, with occasional visits to Prestwick. A new possibility arose in March 1941 for letting the house to a bombed-out firm of estate agents in Mount Street, but this was vetoed by the Grosvenor Estate. In April a bomb fell nearby in the garden of No. 43, but failed to explode. Then in June Lady Ward was given the use of the ground and first floors for the Dudley House Committee, an organisation for the supply of food and other materials from the USA to Britain. When they ceased to require the house as a store in September 1942, it was offered to the Greek Government for use as 'Greek House', in the same way that Mrs Ronnie Greville had made her house in Charles Street available to the Dutch Government in Exile. The stated purpose of Greek House was to provide a centre for the better understanding of the character, history, achievements and cultural heritage of the British and Greek peoples, and to develop closer relations between Greeks resident in the United Kingdom and the British friends of Greece. The British Council, which had made itself responsible for 'the cultural well-being of those subjects of Allied nations who are now in this country', acted as a go-between, and a peppercorn rent was agreed. In November Sotheby's were asked to sell the household china, which rather surprisingly ran to 432 meat-plates, over 200 teacups, saucers and plates, and 140 coffee cups and saucers. The Council members included Anthony Eden, R. A. Butler, Professor Gilbert Murray and two former British Ministers in Athens, Sir Percy Loraine and Sir Michael Palairet, who were also on the Executive Committee. There was an informal opening on 15 December. Alicia also became a member, and Clive paid her subscription of £5. Greek House also bought the carpets and curtains in the house for £577. The Director was D. L. Perkins, who had had some experience of Greece and the Greeks and had been lent by Pearson's when the company was forced by the German invasion to abandon their business there. When he retired at Christmas 1943, Sir Michael Palairet wrote to Clive 'I never enter Greek House without feeling how fortunate we are in having such ideal surroundings for its activities.'

In April 1945 Sir Michael wrote again to Clive asking if there would be a possibility of the house becoming an Anglo-Greek Club when the war was over. Clive replied that 'the idea appeals to me very strongly' but that they had not yet been able to make any plans for its future. The British Council would have no funds to finance Greek House after 31 March 1946. Meanwhile, it was closed for three weeks in September, being handed over to Archbishop Damaskinos, who was Regent of Greece while a plebiscite was held to decide whether or not the king should return to his country.

The next applicants for the lease were an organisation called the Society for Cultural Relations between the Peoples of the British Commonwealth and the USSR, which was given short shrift. By the end of 1945 Clive was actively supporting a drive to increase the club membership so that Greek House could remain in place. This appealed to him partly on general grounds, and partly because he and his family would thereby be able to use the top two floors of the house as a flat, as they eventually did in 1948. Meanwhile a new tenancy for one year was granted in February 1946 to give the club a chance to increase its membership to a viable level. A very characteristic note was struck by Clive when he declined an invitation to take the chair at an evening lecture on hydroelectrics by a Mr Tsirimokos, a former member of Pearson's staff in Athens. Clive had a genuine previous engagement, but apologised for being so unhelpful, 'although, as I disclosed to you, taking the chair is *not* something I enjoy'. He and Alicia each gave guarantees of £100 towards the total of £2,500 which the committee had decided on as a necessary basis for the continuation of the club. They also lent the existing furniture and pictures to the new foundation, including silver candelabra and brackets. In February 1948 the club was granted an extension of its lease for two more years, but it was not destined to survive, largely because the natural abstemiousness of the Greeks prevented the bar from making the necessary profits, and in February 1951 notice was given terminating the lease in June. It was then sold back to the Grosvenor Estate, and to the great sorrow of the family, the house was pulled down a few years later to make room for the new American Embassy. The panelling was sold at Sotheby's for £6,650, though the estimate was for no more than £3,475.

Clive and Alicia then had to find a new London base. Alicia's close friend Lady Wavell, who had lost her only son in the war, and whose husband the Field Marshal had just died, was giving up her flat in Kingston House, Knightsbridge. Out of sympathy, and a characteristic desire to help, Alicia bought the large but rather impersonal flat, and it was afterwards used by most of the family when they were in London.

In the meantime, a great deal had been going on at Parham since 1939. To begin with, there were the universal complications of rationing, of food and clothes and petrol, and the problems of the blackout, which given the size and shape of the windows was a more daunting problem than in most houses. However, expertise at solving practical questions of that kind was second nature to Clive, and soon became so for those who worked for him. Before the war actually broke out, it was known that the evacuees would be coming, and Veronica was sent off from Bembridge, where the family were sailing, to organise the fitting-out of Parham for the war. Ever since the family had moved in sixteen years before, the house had been in a state of flux while alterations were made. Different rooms had been used for eating and sitting in at different times, but now there was a fresh upheaval on a bigger scale than ever. The human ups and downs were still more taxing. There sprung up at Parham a permanent floating house-party of a size in proportion to the house. It consisted first of Captain Sir Bryan Godfrey-Faussett, a former naval equerry to King George V, who had been bombed out of his grace and favour house, the Ranger's Lodge in Hyde Park. He and his wife were old family friends, and together with her maid and an exceptionally demanding Siamese cat, they moved into Parham for the duration of the war. Also came another friend of Alicia, the novelist Susan Ertz, who had married Major Ronald McCrindle, the former managing director of British Airways. He was away at BOAC – from whom he eventually parted company – during the week, but spent weekends at Parham during the early part of the war. Leslie Runciman described him as

getting extremely impatient with his staff, and taking no pains to conceal it; he despises the arts of making oneself liked to such an extent that it sometimes looks as if he were going out of his way to do the opposite. He has always been disliked by his staff, and so far as he is aware of it or cares about it, almost glories in the fact ... preferring to give an instruction or expect it to be obeyed from a sense of discipline rather than make any outward effort to carry the man concerned with him.'

Next came Clive's Aunt Arab, Mrs Charles Camm, who was the less favoured of Lady Cowdray's two sisters, complete with her maid and Rolls-Royce and chauffeur, who would report for orders every morning at eleven, irrespective of the fact that the petrol ration would not run to more than a monthly expedition to Worthing. Then came Miss McQueen, who had been Alicia's governess in Rome in the 1890s, and although of an angelic disposition was accompanied by an extremely bossy younger sister. When Clive appeared at Parham, after much work and long, slow and uncomfortable journeys, he would invariably put his copy of *The Times* on the table reserved for papers in the Great Hall; whereupon the younger Miss McQueen would officiously spring to her feet and offer him her own copy of *The Times*. Exasperated by the innumerable repetitions of this absurd scene, one day Clive courteously and solemnly handed over his own copy in exchange for hers, and the performance was never repeated.

Another couple who spent their weekends at Parham, though busy with war work in London during the week, were Charlie Phillips and his wife Trix. They had become close friends of the Pearsons after what might seem an unpromising start. In 1932 Clive and Alicia had taken Veronica and the present Lord Cowdray, together with Mr Body, on a visit to Mexico, where they had been treated more or less as visiting heads of state. Their general manager in Mexico City, Bill Davies, obligingly moved out of his house to accommodate them, and it was suggested to the Phillips's, who lived in the adjoining house but had no connection with Pearson's, that they might like to move out as well. Furthermore, to make quite sure that the visitors would not feel cramped in any way, a gap was made in the hedge between the gardens of the two houses. Nevertheless, they all became close friends, and Trix Phillips, who was a cultivated woman and shared a love of music with Alicia, came to the rescue and helped with social arrangements when Veronica came out. She and her husband had been marooned on one of these visits at the time when war broke out. They were thought to have done rather well by coming back to England for the war, even if accidentally, and being homeless were naturally taken in at Parham. To round off the party there was an exceedingly dignified retired housekeeper of Lady Cowdray's from Paddockhurst, together with her still-room maid Maggie, who had been accustomed to getting up at five o'clock every morning to make the croissants for breakfast, and, like others, found some difficulty in acclimatising herself to the wartime regime.

At the other end of the house were billeted another party of thirty small boys, aged from four to ten, who had been evacuated from a school in Peckham with two or three teachers from a girl's school, to whom the boys were at first strangers. However, on arrival at Parham by bus from Pulborough station they careered round the grounds until they reached the Round Pond. Catching sight of some elderly goldfish cruising in it, one of them, a natural leader, cried out in delight 'Ooh look, Miss, bloaters!', and the entire party began to thrash the water with any offensive weapon they could lay their hands on. Somehow the goldfish were reprieved, and on his next visit Clive was so delighted by the boys' excitement at being in the country for the first time that he had a large wooden hut built for them in the garden, with the roof thatched with heather.

The main purpose of this was no doubt to reduce the likelihood of their getting up to mischief in the house, but he also had a long flower-bed divided up into vegetable plots, which the boys cultivated in pairs, and which soon came to be a source of great enjoyment to them. Food production was intensified in the walled garden, and Veronica still remembers the unpleasant task of picking endless frosted brussels sprouts on a field opposite the lake, grimly referred to as the 'Convicts' Plot'.

Somehow the hungry population of the house was fed, by means of a fluctuating and often strange assortment of domestic staff. Alicia spent endless time and trouble on the needs of the refugees, and on the whims of their parents who would sometimes turn up and announce that 'Mr Brown doesn't think Hitler's going to do any bombing after all so we've decided to take the kiddies home again after dinner'. She always somehow provided lunch for those parents who came to visit their children on Sundays, but soon had to make a rule that once removed they could not be brought back, otherwise the use of Parham as a kind of free hotel would have made arrangements that were already very difficult completely impossible.

Ten days after the war broke out, Lavinia had married Michael Smiley in the little church on the other side of the lawn at Parham. He was a joint master of the Cowdray Hunt, and a captain in the Rifle Brigade. After a hideous period of uncertainty when he was reported missing at Calais, it became known that he had been taken prisoner. Much later, he succeeded in escaping. Their daughter Miranda was born in August 1940, and to the comfort of Alicia, Lavinia spent the rest of the war based at Parham, helping with the huge influx of humanity. Veronica had also married early in the war, but her husband Marcus Rueff, a gifted and much-liked publisher, was killed in North Africa less than a year later, serving with the Tower Hamlets Rifles (9th Battalion, the Rifle Brigade). While the threat of German invasion lasted in 1940, Parham was in the general area in which it was likely to strike, but most of the time the inhabitants of Parham were too busy with their new task of housekeeping for numbers that were to vary between seventy and ninety to have much time for worrying about the threat. An elaborate rota was established for fire-watching, with its headquarters in the Great Hall, also the scene of large-scale knitting of khaki socks and gloves and Balaclava helmets. To prevent a general degeneration into a flood of wool, Clive had a special table set up for the materials used in these occupations. Apart from baby clothes, which were considered acceptable, the only exception to war-related work was the decision of Lady Godfrey-Faussett to embark on painting a set of what were hailed as very pretty table mats copied from some Sèvres china that she had brought with her. Cridland would occasionally appear to inform Clive about 'Vera Lynn, sir, just coming on' on the wireless, or occasionally either 'Air Raid warning red' or its opposite 'Air Raid warning white', indicating the All Clear, but delivered in exactly the same indifferent tone of voice.

Occasionally Miranda was able to have a child of her own age to stay, and in 1942 it was even possible for Lavinia to take her to the seaside at Bognor, a few miles away, which although still barricaded with barbed wire made a pleasant change. One afternoon there was an air raid, and one of the other children, who was terrified of thunder, was heard being reassured by her mother: 'Don't worry, Jane, it's not thunder, it's only bombs.' In the same year, the evacuees finally returned to Peckham, and were replaced by troops of the Canadian Third Corps, who were training for their later part in the invasion of Europe. Veronica was by this time running the estate office, after a crash course in management consisting of a single week with her cousin Judy Burrell at Knepp Castle nearby. She was also put in charge of arrangements for the HQ company of the Canadians, who were billeted in the house, and as she did not conceal the fact that she alone was in a position to obtain extra fuel for them as well as controlling their supplies of food and hot water, harmonious relations were soon established. Their training included the mending of bridges under water, and Veronica would be invited to join them in marching round the bottom of the swimming-pool equipped with a gas-mask, into which air was pumped from a compressor on the bank, a snorkel, and boots and belt weighed down with lead.

The Canadians established themselves in three field companies, each in its own huts in the park, with the headquarter company billeted in the house, occupying the Great Hall and everything to the west of it. An ammunition dump was set up in the big sand pit facing the east end of the house, and a welfare and recreation department was set up in a vast Nissen hut. On two or three evenings a week Veronica and Lavinia would be on duty there, helping with letters home and providing stamps and also arranging accommodation where the troops could spend their leaves, usually in Hove, Brighton or Worthing. The YMCA and Salvation Army were particularly helpful, and various small hotels had their existence enlivened in this way. The two sisters would sit under a large notice displaying the word INFORMATION in large letters. Visiting them on one occasion to inspect the department, Clive said cheerfully 'I don't know how you have the nerve.' But nerve had increased on all sides with the progress of the war, and Parham and its various departments was no exception. The last troops did not leave their camp until late in 1946, when their huts were eventually swept away, though their foundations, and the access roads leading to them, remain there to this day.

Dione meanwhile worked for a time as a billeting officer under Mrs

Toby Fitzwilliam in Petworth, and would set off every morning on a bicycle ingeniously fitted with a small but spirited engine attached to the handlebars. After a few weeks this dreary work palled, and she embarked on a secretarial course in London which would lead to work in the Political Intelligence Department of the Foreign Office. Before the war started, she had studied acting and had earned several parts on the professional stage. Her parents, unlike most others would have done, encouraged and supported her enthusiastically.

Two chicken runs, called Greater Parham and Chicken Villa, were built on the lawn outside the South Library, formerly the site of two grass tennis courts. With Clive based in London in the week, working away in drab wartime conditions, Alicia somehow contrived to spend two or three days a week with him there, and she herself worked in the canteen in the National Gallery. Though denuded of many of its treasures, which were taken to North Wales for safety, it became the setting for a series of lunchtime concerts inspired by the Director, Kenneth Clark: many great musicians performed there, including Myra Hess. With entertainment of all kinds much curtailed, and night-life in particular hampered by the blackout and other restrictions, these concerts provided inspiration and uplift, and generally did a lot for morale. The canteen played its part, and many sandwiches were cut up and filled with dubious fish paste. Alicia was both horrified and amused, on arriving for work one morning and opening the knife-drawer, to see a very large rat jump out after spending a happy night among the crumbs. But when she was at Parham, Alicia's war work included removing the heavy buckets of chicken manure from the runs and transferring them to the refugee children's gardens, a task which must have reminded her nose of dutiful visits to the equally repellent nitrate fields of Chile twenty years earlier. However, in these stressful circumstances she became much attached to her thirty Rhode Island Red and Light Sussex hens, though carrying the heavy buckets eventually brought on painful fibrositis, and her labours were restricted on her doctor's orders.

Alicia had always been loyal to an exceptional degree, perhaps commoner then than now, in accepting conditions of life which she would not have chosen for herself. Her greatest disappointment was in not bearing Clive a son, but there was compensation in plenty in the unusually close, sympathetic and loving relationships which she established with her daughters, of whom Lavinia was probably the closest in temperament. Over the years, she also had the satisfaction of seeing

Parham transformed, largely through her steady efforts, from a forlorn, empty, barn-like shell into a family home filled with treasures, which she modestly pretended that the house collected of its own accord. In fact, of course, her scholarship and appetite for research went far beyond the usual amateur range, to the extent that A. L. Rowse urged her, after a visit to Parham, to write a short life of the Elizabethan Lord Zouche, adding in a letter 'Please don't be alarmed by my suggestion: you would find it such fun and so interesting.' She must also have felt rewarded by the letters that she received from the mothers of the evacuee children, some of which arrived as much as twenty years later, at the time of Miranda Smiley's engagement. One wrote 'You will never know what it has meant to me to know my son has been so well cared for'; another, 'I always had that secure sort of feeling that George was safe while under your care'. One of the boys, after returning to Peckham, wrote simply 'I miss you all very much'. Certainly, at this difficult time, her gentleness, humility, untiring energy and original sense of humour must have been called on to the limit. Clive had always set her a practical and effective example: he expected her to follow it, and follow it she did.

9
Last Years

When the war was finally over in August 1945, the conditions of peace were to remain austere and in many ways grim for several years to come. As far as the care of large, old houses was concerned, many of their owners gave up in despair or moved out for other reasons. The huge public interest in them that was to spring up later was quite unforeseeable, and, as it turned out, Parham was to be one of the pioneers in creating it. Most large houses had been neglected during the war to some degree, and if they had been used for wartime purposes, as was nearly always the case, their state was often extremely discouraging. The building industry was immediately, and not unreasonably, concentrated on the replacement of houses and factories and other buildings that had been destroyed in the war – 60,000 in the blitz in 1940 and 1941, and over 10,000 by flying bombs in 1944. For anything like ordinary improvements or redecorations a crippling licensing scheme was soon introduced, under which it was illegal, as well as unpatriotic, to carry out work costing more than £25 in any one year.

Thanks in part to Veronica's firm diplomacy with the Canadians, and the general spirit of unselfishness that had prevailed at Parham during the war, it was spared the full horrors of occupation. Staircases had not been torn out and used for firewood, and Vandykes had not been turned into makeshift dartboards, as happened elsewhere. Altogether, the house was luckier than many, partly also because Clive himself had been at hand intermittently to keep an eye on things wherever possible. But the prospect of living in it again, even on a much reduced scale, with the children grown up and gone, was daunting. (Dione had married, in July 1945, Patrick Gibson, who joined the Westminster Press, became a director of the *Financial Times*, chairman of Pearson's when Lord Cowdray retired, and later in life was made a life peer and served successively as Chairman of the Arts Council and the National Trust, as well as filling a number of other important positions in the cultural establishment.) The wedding was at Parham, and Veronica remembers the amiable Canadians clearing debris out of the church beforehand, while their unecclesiastical songs floated across the lawn in clouds of cigarette smoke. Michael Smiley had escaped after nearly five years in German prison camps, and on his return he and Lavinia had wanted to settle and farm within reach of Parham. But there, as in many other fields, demand exceeded supply, and when Clive offered them Castle Fraser they made their home there, though neither of them had till then had more than brief holiday connections with Scotland.

Veronica, who had acquired considerable experience of general management at Parham in the war years, remained there for the time being as Clive's invaluable lieutenant. But in an increasingly servantless and inflationary age, what was to be done with the house? Fortunately, a heaven-sent figure now appeared on the horizon in the shape of Rupert Gunnis. His chief living memorial is his *Dictionary of English Sculptors*, but although his first passion was for the rediscovery of forgotten and neglected works by Nollekens and Rysbrack in churches all over the country, his enthusiasm and historical curiosity extended over a far wider field. Summed up by John Cornforth in his articles on Parham in *Country Life* as 'independent, entertaining, knowledgeable and energetic', he lived at Tunbridge Wells, not far from the eastern border of Sussex, and happened to meet the Pearsons one day at lunch with neighbours. Becoming aware of his interests, they suggested that next time he was passing he might like to come and see Parham. When they got home, the door bell rang, and there was Rupert Gunnis, asking if it would be convenient for him to see over the house that very afternoon. It was somehow typical of Clive's judgement and of the good luck that it sometimes earned him, that in spite of a great difference in temperament he immediately took to this exuberant stranger, who might best be described as one of the last of the dedicated gentleman scholars. Clive and Alicia came to the conclusion that the house should be arranged, as far as possible, to make a chronological story, so that its history could be explained and understood largely through the portraits that had been assembled there; and this decision, as has been seen, led to further purchases in order to fill in gaps in the collection of portraits connected in some way or other with the house. Rupert Gunnis was also engaged in advising the owners of Castle Howard on the task of opening it to the public, and when this eventually came to pass in August 1952 George Howard, the owner, sent Alicia the following telegram. 'Castle Howard presents humble duty to Parham and begs to report that owing to benevolent tutelage score 1420 Sunday and Monday stop Rupert footless and voiceless Howard.' George Howard was so grateful to Parham that he later wrote to Alicia 'You were our godparent.'

As the work of rearrangement went on at Parham, weekend visitors were constantly pressed into service to help with picture-hanging and furniture-moving, and, as Veronica saw it, nothing short of producing a medical certificate would have excused them from work, which, through infectious enthusiasm, soon of course became a pleasure as well. But after Rupert Gunnis himself began to pay regular visits, his servant refused to allow him to take his better clothes with him to Parham, because they always became so dirty there. At first, however, both Clive and Alicia had been astonished by his immediate suggestion that the house should be opened. Their characteristically modest reaction was 'It's not a famous house, who on earth would want to come and see it?' But they were persuaded that almost without noticing it, they had turned it over the years into a showpiece with a strong, individual character of its own, first by restoring it physically into something like its original plan, and then by filling it, step by step, with exactly the kind of contents that suited it best, historically as well as aesthetically. All their misgivings yielded to the eagerness and encouragement of Rupert Gunnis, who first stayed at Parham in February 1947, and the wheels were set in motion. Not only were organisation and planning dear to Clive's heart for their own sake, out of the habits of a lifetime, but the plan was to solve, neatly, two separate problems: first, the future of the house, and further ahead, his retirement from the family business.

He cannot have felt inclined, except out of a sense of responsibility, to adapt himself at the age of sixty to the new conditions of a post-war Labour Government, and its unforeseeable impact on the world of business, particularly as regards nationalisation, of which he had already had bitter experience both at the Southern Railway and BOAC. He gradually urged his nephew to form his own group of advisers and directors and to run the Pearson group in his own way, which he was to do with outstanding success with the help of talented new blood such as that of Oliver Poole. At the end of 1949 Clive would resign as a director of Lazards and as chairman of several of the Pearson subsidiaries, including Whitehall Securities, Whitehall Electric, and the two Greek companies, Société Générale Hellénique and Athens Piraeus Electricity. But until 1954 he remained a director of the Cowdray Trust and, most important of all, stayed firmly in the chair at Pearson's itself, carefully monitoring the progress of all the companies in the group, and ultimately still taking most of the important decisions himself. But he was certainly not one to interfere after his retirement, though Pat Gibson remembers one penetrating comment that he made when consulted at the time of the Suez Crisis in 1956. His only recommendation was that the Government should 'keep calm and not upset the Arabs'. He had had more than enough of politics and politicians in the war, and even in a great national crisis would never have sought to influence public policy of his own accord, but it is certainly more than a pity that his simple formula was not followed by Eden.

As soon as building regulations were relaxed in the 1950s, the Long Gallery at Parham was slightly remodelled, as always with the intention of restoring it as near as possible to its original form. The top floor of the Square Tower next to the front door (which had been added in Robert Curzon's time) was taken down, making it possible to reinstate one of the two north-facing windows in the Long Gallery which had been blocked up and fitted with a fireplace. Panelling on all the small window bays was also pushed back so that the window recesses let in more light. The Victorian treatment of the ceiling had also by now become damaged by leaks, and much thought was given to its replacement. Other galleries of the same date, Chastleton and Burton Agnes, were studied for inspiration. Eventually a bold design was commissioned from Oliver Messel, whose stage sets for various operas at Glyndebourne had strongly appealed to Veronica, and whose family had been established in Sussex for a hundred years. After various false starts Messel designed a plan in five sections, with a scheme of painted foliage running over the divisions. Afterwards the paint began to flake, but by then Messel had moved to the West Indies, and a successor, Gordon Davies, was called in. Alicia happened to show him some of the colour-plate books in her collection, and between them they incorporated birds and butterflies into the foliage, so that, to quote John Cornforth again, 'the effect is of walking through a tunnel of trellis in an exotic Elizabethan garden'. Opinions about its real merits vary, but it is certainly a good example of the absence of academic pedantry in the way in which the Pearsons treated the house, and of the important part played in it by their own personal ideas. John Cornforth accurately sums up all these alterations and improvements all over the house as 'an extraordinary, sensitive and individual essay in historical imagination'. A bust of Alicia's mother, Lady Brabourne, by the Serbian sculptor Mestrovic, had already been placed there together with a sketchier bronze of Alicia herself by the same artist. A charming needlework picture by Lady Brabourne also now hangs there, looking as if it is at least two hundred years old. In fact it depicts Clive and Alicia, as the new owners of Parham shortly after its acquisition, dressed in seventeenth century clothes, with Veronica toddling at their feet.

Lady Brabourne had been a keen needleworker and collector of needlework, much of which remains at Parham. She also had an exceptional gift for story-telling, and her grandchildren regarded her as an almost magical figure, partly as a result of the wonderful tales which she invented and told them, each day's invention following on from the day before. Her early death in 1929 had been a particularly sad blow to the family.

But before most of these improvements could be embarked on, guides had to be selected and trained so that the house could be shown to visitors to best advantage. Nowhere perhaps is Alicia's thoughtfulness, intelligence, taste and common sense shown more clearly than in the instructions which she composed for the guides, and which deserve to be quoted in full.

Notes for Guides on How to Show a House to Visitors

(1) FOREWORD The principal reason of showing Parham is that people may have an opportunity of seeing and appreciating for themselves the beauty and interest of an Elizabethan house and its value as a record of the past.

An old building needs constant supervision and expenditure to keep it in repair. However massive a structure may appear, yet beams decay, mortar crumbles, stones loosen and bricks fall away. The rooms, planned to suit a way of life long passed, seldom lend themselves to conversion into a modern institution. It is more likely, when private means fail, that the building will be allowed to lapse into ruin or be scheduled for destruction.

We hope that those who visit Parham may be encouraged to feel that it is reasonable, and even important, that England's heritage of old houses shall be preserved. Well-informed and sympathetic guides can do much to assist this cause.

(2) THE PUBLIC There are, of course, many types and classes of visitors. It is an art to adapt oneself to the party in hand, providing the kind of information that is most likely to appeal to them.

In a mixed party one should remember that the educated already know enough to be interested in what they see, but the entertainment of the uneducated – and possibly bored – depends a great deal upon the guide. If you can arouse interest and appreciation in the simpler people, you will have done a more useful and rewarding piece of work than if you were to discourse to a few cultured members in the party.

People of limited education will almost certainly be interested to hear about the manner of life 300 years ago. They will like to know the uses to which the various rooms were put, and to see portraits of the people who lived in them. Needlework and tapestry usually appeal to the women; while furniture and clocks – and particularly the kinds of wood of which these things are made – are of interest to the men.

As for the more sophisticated, it has sometimes happened that a party has said on arrival 'Oh, must we have a guide? We had rather not', and on their departure have been heard to remark to each other that the guide had contributed much to their enjoyment of the tour.

In fact, enthusiasm is infectious, and if you are interested yourself and equipped with a variety of information to draw upon, you will probably find an angle to suit even the most unresponsive.

(3) FAULTS TO AVOID There are two principal pitfalls in guiding, each equally easy to fall into.

Dullness The recitation of facts in a voice that has become monotonous from repetition. This may be corrected by varying the pitch or the volume of your voice from time to time. Also by choosing different pictures and objects about which to talk.

Facetiousness In an attempt to make the tour light and enjoyable to the public, it is a fault to overdo the gaiety and relapse into slangy talk. This is apt to give the impression that what the public may have come far to see is quite unimportant and trivial.

It is possible to treat the entertaining and the inspiring aspects of history so that both are equally interesting.

For example, so great a personality as Queen Elizabeth should be treated with respect. Her human foibles can be touched upon, but her transcendent qualities of statesmanship and devotion to duty should be stressed.

(4) INFORMATION The points of interest in the house, pictures and furniture, and detailed information upon them, are available in 'the dictionary' and guides need to refresh their memory from these sheets from time to time.

(5) TIMETABLE The most convenient route to take in the course of showing each room has been worked out, and the sketch plans should be studied.

Keep strictly to the times allotted to the various rooms, otherwise the parties ahead and behind you will suffer.

If, owing to interest shown by a visitor, more time than usual has to be devoted to a particular thing, on no account hurry through all the rest, but omit mention of something else to which you generally call attention. This adjustment comes naturally with practice.

A large party tends to move slowly and takes longer to look about. It is, therefore, wise to tell them less and point out fewer things.

(6) POSITION, MANNER AND DELIVERY Stand to one side of the picture or object that you are showing and face your audience. You can then see whether you are interesting them, and whether a wanderer is doing anything he should not.

On leaving one room for another pass out last, so as to see that no one is left behind.

Take for granted that your audience is going to be interested. Be friendly but not undignified. Neither condescending nor dictatorial. And never, never, facetious.

Above all be audible. Speak clearly and not too fast. Do not attempt to say all you know about each thing.

(7) CONVERSATIONS AND QUESTIONS Avoid conversations. They are often difficult to stop, but unless the visitor is giving you valuable information much of other people's time is wasted.

Answer questions as briefly as you can and loud enough for all to hear. It is useful, for the sake of those who may not have heard the question, to embody it in your reply.

Example. Q. Is that table walnut?
A. No, it is made of oak.

Never be inaccurate. If you do not know the answer offer to find it out before they leave. And look it up in the West Library.

(8) GENERAL Make a point of going round with other guides, and note what parts of the script they use. Everyone naturally has a different approach and there are good hints to be picked up from all.

This also gives you an opportunity of feeling what it is like to be a member of a conducted party.

(9) Remember that it is much more tiring for your audience than it is for you, so be concise in your statements and use no unnecessary verbosity.

(10) Let your movements in each room be according to plan. Go to each pre-arranged station and remain quietly there; do not wander up and down.

(11) Remember that in a large party those at the back cannot see you or your gestures, so describe the location of the object: viz., 'the picture over the fireplace', 'the sampler above the lamp', etc.

(12) Speak with authority, but be ready to admit ignorance if asked something you do not know. Offer to provide the answer later. (See also last paragraph No. 7).

(13) Very rarely does a visitor give any trouble, but the following need special attention:–

The Touchers who finger needlework, tapestry and even paintings, must be called to order at once. It is possible to do this pleasantly, by using such a phrase as 'I am so sorry, but I have to ask you not to touch.'

The Wanderers who do not listen to you, are often people who have been before and want to examine certain things more closely. But, since some may be untrustworthy characters, you should keep them within your range of vision.

The Deaf can be encouraged to stand close to you, though if this is useless let them wander, but keep an eye on them. It is tiring both to you and the rest of the party if you shout all the time. Remember that many can lip read, and be sure to face your audience. (See also first paragraph, No. 6).

Children. Try from time to time to produce a story, or point out a detail that will interest any child in the party.

The Inquisitive who want to know the number of staff kept, the name of their last guide, etc., etc., are best put off by pleading ignorance. 'I am afraid I cannot tell you.'

Alicia was particularly rewarded by various remarks made by visitors and remembered by the guides. They are all the more interesting for coming from a time when country-house visiting by the public was a new pastime, and impressions were often fresher and more original, and for having been made spontaneously, rather than self-consciously written down in a visitors' book. Always encouraging from Alicia's point of view, and often repeated in a variety of other forms, was the comment that Parham was 'so different from the "Museum" houses. It will always be in the family, won't it? I mean, the Government won't get it?' 'How lovely it all is – and not a school or anything dreadful', which was particularly ironic in view of the schoolchildren that had been cared for there in the war. Other remarks were more unexpected: 'We often start to go to Arundel, but we always come here', and 'This is my tenth visit. I bring all my Australian friends.' But often they were of a more distinctively personal kind, expressing the true feelings of the individual: 'These pictures are like a meal to me.' 'These paintings stand right out and hit you.' 'It's extraordinary. You come here for the sake of the ladies, expecting to be bored, and you go away delighted.' A small boy was heard to ask 'Is this house alive, Mummy?', and a stout old gentleman, gazing at the portrait of Lady Hamilton, reflected 'How I wish I'd been Lord Nelson . . .' But of all the comments, the two which perhaps gave Alicia the greatest pleasure were from a lady who said to her companion 'Do you see, dear, they are not only greenhouse flowers, but primroses and cowslips from the fields?'; and best of all, when Alicia herself was on duty as a guide, a visitor who had been inspecting a group of rather stolid and unprepossessing Bysshopp portraits asked her 'Is the present owner very plain too?' Only occasionally was a critical note heard, as in the case of a man who complained 'This house is far too modern. Give me Penshurst every time.' Later on, by the time Veronica had inherited the house, a well-informed visitor was heard to say 'Mrs Tritton is a subsidiary Pearson, you know.'

About this time a curious episode occurred which shows Clive at his most loyal, generous and, as usual, discreet. His friend from Cambridge days, Toby Fitzwilliam, who had become a neighbour in Sussex, was suddenly called on to face an extraordinary public ordeal. He had been brought up as the eldest son of his father, and his twenty-first birthday, which Clive attended, had been celebrated in 1909 at one of the family homes, Milton in Northamptonshire, in keeping with 'what was to be expected on the coming of age of a large landed proprietor'. His mother had died in 1925 and until his father's death in 1935 he believed he would inherit the Milton estate, but then discovered that everything had been left to his younger brother, who eventually also became the tenth and last Earl Fitzwilliam. All he had from the family was £1,000 a year.

The cause of this bombshell was the fact that it was by no means clear that his father had married his mother, who had been a minor actress, before Toby Fitzwilliam's birth. To clear the air and establish the succession, it was agreed by all concerned to settle the question in the courts and Toby Fitzwilliam reluctantly made a legal petition for a declaration of legitimacy. The situation had been brought to a head by the death in an air crash of the 8th Earl Fitzwilliam. His cousin, the 9th Earl, had no children, so that Toby and his brother, who was sixteen years younger and was then unmarried, were the next heirs. Toby was the only member of the Fitzwilliam family to have male descendants (a son and a grandson) to carry on the line, and if Toby had not taken this step himself the family trustees would have been obliged to take it on their own account in order to deal with the trust property for which they were responsible. He behaved in an exemplary fashion from beginning to end. Before the case began he wrote to Clive 'As you know my heart has never been in this matter but I took it up in the first place so that my family could never blame me for letting an opportunity slip by for want of a little enterprise and trouble . . . The chances of being able to refund any of the costs of a trial are negligible except in the unlikely event of our winning the case.' He was at first legally advised by Sir Walter Monckton, a brilliant lawyer who had served as Solicitor-General in Churchill's caretaker Government at the end of the war, and later as Minister of Labour, and of Defence. However, he was obliged to drop the case in order to fight a by-election and enter the House of Commons. His place was taken by a no less distinguished advocate in the form of Sir David Maxwell Fyfe, who was afterwards, as Lord Kilmuir, Lord Chancellor. Toby Fitzwilliam commented drily that his new counsel had 'disposed brilliantly of Ribbentrop & Co. at Nuremberg, though how much the two cases have in common remains to be seen'.

It is enough to say that after a long case in court, stridently reported in the press, it was held that Toby's parents had not been married when he was born. Clive had undertaken to pay his costs, which finally amounted to over £10,000, and the letter of thanks that he received afterwards deserves to be quoted:

Never, do I suppose, has any friendship been tried so highly as yours to me, and never can one have remained so firm through all the trials it has been put through since those far off days at Cambridge. Your support of me and those who were advising me during the past months has put a really wonderful crown on it all.

I must admit I am surprised after listening to all the evidence the judge's not accepting that my parents ever intended to get married in Scotland and much less succeeded in doing so. But one has to realise that a judge has all the training to assess the evidence at its true value and the neutral spirit to set aside all prejudices which is very difficult for the parties concerned. My faith in British justice is in no way shaken.

He died four years after the case.

Besides the opening of the house, which inevitably affected daily life at Parham considerably but also provided a constant source of interest not least as a financial operation, other changes were going ahead. In 1945 the Home Farm only amounted to 400 acres, but by 1947, with the retirement of a number of tenants on the adjoining farms, Clive was farming 2,500 acres in hand, with land at Springhead, Wiggonholt and Kithurst all run side by side under a single manager.

By contrast with the embarrassments of the Fitzwilliam case, there was rejoicing at Parham at the marriage of Veronica in 1950 to Paddy Tritton, who had become a close friend of the family through sailing activities in the last years before the war, in which he served throughout in the Navy. He was now a partner in the stockbroking firm of Heseltine Moss, and he and Veronica settled at Monks, an agreeable house at Paddockhurst. To Clive's relief, they now took charge of the estate there, and Paddy Tritton's keen interest in forestry and shooting gave the task a special attraction for him. When they bought the main house after the first Lady Cowdray's death, the Benedictines had been well advised, and had acquired with it 500 acres of farmland in the centre of the estate, but in 1950 Clive had redressed the balance by acquiring from the estate of Lady Wentworth at Crabbet a further 640 acres on the boundary of the Paddockhurst property nearest to what was to become Crawley New Town, thereby not only gaining a buffer against the town, but also a stretch of land that might one day be of greatly increased value if planning policy were ever altered. In 1987 forty acres of this were sure enough sold for development, after the building of the M23 motorway, thus making it possible to secure the estate in the hands of three of the sons of Pat and

Dione Gibson, and enabling them to buy out their Smiley cousins. Veronica, sadly having no children of her own, was thus able to divide the estate to which she and her husband had devoted so much time and trouble equally for the benefit of the next generation. The new area was in a sad state, consisting of derelict woodland that had been felled during the war. But Clive established a scheme for replanting at the rate of thirty acres a year, very much sustained by the enthusiasm of Paddy Tritton. The soil is light and sandy, which limited the varieties of timber that would flourish; but larch, Norway and sitka spruce, Scots pine and Spanish chestnut have been grown successfully. The new woods were planted in sections separated by broad rides which act as fire-breaks as well as improving the shooting, and at the time of writing are steadily recovering from the effects of the devastating hurricane of October 1987. At the junction of two of the principal rides, a fine specimen of Nothofagus, the Chilean Beech, has been planted and labelled in memory of Paddy Tritton, and will in due course become a notable landmark. Among other local activities, the Trittons organised a visit to the estate by the Royal Forestry Society in 1960, when the results of Clive's planting scheme over the years were much admired. The woods were also awarded a series of prizes by the Southern Counties Agricultural Society. Not far from the Tritton Memorial Tree can be seen the foundations of a woodland retreat built by Lady Wentworth's father, the poet and adventurer Wilfrid Scawen Blunt. It was his family that had been the owners of the Crabbet estate, and he had earlier taken part in a series of quasi-historical revels at Parham as a guest of the Zouches in the 1870s.

A feature of Clive's life in retirement at Parham after this time was the game of croquet, to which he was introduced by Major Jack Abbey, who lived only three miles away and who had already provided Alicia with much encouragement and help in the field of book collecting. Major Abbey also thought that a pair of peacocks would enhance the gardens at Parham, but after they had been introduced there they did so much damage to the flower-beds and exasperated Clive to such a degree with their mournful cries, especially at dawn, that he came to the conclusion that they would be better suited at Cowdray, among the ruins of the medieval castle. They were therefore installed there (a difficult present to decline) but for some reason took a dislike to their new surroundings and very surprisingly succeeded in making their way, chiefly on foot rather than on the wing, back to Parham, a distance of over ten miles.

Apart from the liaison with Castle Howard, the curators of stately homes in the early days of their opening to the public corresponded with each other in suitably stately language, echoing the ambassadors of the Renaissance. A letter has survived at Parham from Hatfield, as follows: 'Following the pleasant and, as I believe, mutually beneficial custom which has grown up in recent years between our two houses, I have pleasure in sending you, under separate cover, a supply of our leaflets'. And nearer home, there were other collaborations when Batemans (Rudyard Kipling's house in Sussex) and the Duchess of Northumberland's house, Albury Park, near Guildford, were opened to the public.

Meanwhile the growth in the number of visitors who paid to see the house followed the pattern of many other successful Pearson projects: a steady, though not uniform, increase from a carefully prepared base. The house was first opened in 1948, on thirty-seven days between July and September, and there were 2,270 visitors; in the next year, on 101 days, 4,585; in 1950, on 106 days, 7,979, partly no doubt thanks to the abolition of petrol rationing; in 1951, on 115 days, 10,752; and in 1953, after a slight drop in between, there were 12,410 on only 108 days. Thereafter, the number of days when the house was open was reduced to a level which varied between 77 and 97, and by 1972, helped by a fair, there was a record number of 27,862 visitors. In the next ten years, to 1983, the totals fluctuated between 24,879 (1973) and 31,954 (1980). In 1983 the house was temporarily closed, but reopened again on a reduced scale in 1985, once again with satisfactory attendance figures.

In the middle of all the hard work and excitement of opening the house, Clive became a victim of cancer of the prostate, diagnosed in 1954, whereupon he gave up the chairmanship of Pearson's. For the next eight years, however, he was able to continue leading a fairly normal life. Various courses of medicine and pills were prescribed for him, one of which made it undesirable for him to have an anaesthetic on a visit to the dentist. When Alicia reminded him of this when he was setting out for an appointment, and advised him to inform the dentist, his answer was characteristic: 'Why should I tell him? Let him find out for himself.' Any encroachment on the activities of someone who was a professional practitioner in his own right was (at least in theory) out of the question.

In 1958 a ball was held for Miranda Smiley, with a marquee specially designed with the intention that it should be used thereafter for local purposes. To Clive's annoyance this afterwards proved to be impossible, but in every other way the ball was a huge success. Soon afterwards Clive's state of health was deteriorating, and in August 1960 Alicia wrote to Lavinia about a worrying attack of vertigo that he had suffered on a visit to an osteopath in Hove: he had been unable to lift his head or to stand, and went home in an ambulance. Five days later he was walking again, but by 1962 he was seriously ill. The marriage of his 'favourite granddaughter' (as he always called Miranda, even though he had no others) to Lord Elveden in that year was a great source of pleasure, and a much-needed tonic to him. Even when confined to his room, he still kept an eagle eye on any estate work that could be observed from his window, and there was no falling-off of standards. He died on 22 July 1965, and was buried, under the simplest gravestone imaginable, outside the little church two hundred yards from the house.

In 1967 Alicia moved out of the main house into a sunny flat on the first floor of the original laundry block, facing south across Fountain Court to the front door, through which she had the satisfaction of seeing the still growing number of 'her' visitors trooping in on the open days. When Clive died, one of those who worked there wrote in a letter of sympathy 'The fact that he was in the house and that we were working for him made it feel as though he was still working with us.' This feeling was to continue in abundance for the next few years, and when the house was open Alicia would prepare twenty-five vases of flowers a week, and frequently took duty as a guide in the Long Gallery. She had the comfort of having Veronica and Paddy Tritton at hand after they moved into Parham, and she continued to visit the flat in Kingston House, on visits to exhibitions, family occasions and the irresistible lure of the saleroom and of antiquarian book dealers such as Quaritch and Maggs. A good example of her continued vigour was her eager acceptance of an invitation from her neighbour Lady Catherine Ashburnham to an 'antiquarian aquatic party, to search the river for broken moulds of Sussex iron firebacks.'

She survived Clive by ten years, more contented and far less empty years than the widowhood of prominent men of affairs often bring. When she died, with merciful suddenness, many letters referred to her 'exceptional charm, intelligence and kindness'. Her personality, all though her life, often made an impression that was immediate as well as long-lasting not only on her own contemporaries but right down to those of her grandchildren as well. Diana Tennant, a cousin of the Pearsons' old friend John Quilter, met her for the first time on one of her last holidays with the family in Venice, and wrote to Lavinia on Alicia's death: 'Never in all my experience has so much respect and affection built up in such a short time... everyone who met her wanted to serve her, and to that end produced their very best.' And Rosemary Courcier, Clive's secretary who had been the great prop of their last years, wrote that Alicia was 'a constant inspiration to all who were fortunate enough to know her – and therefore to love and admire her. She was unique in her selflessness and I shall find it hard to stop grieving.' On top of these deep and widely influential qualities, her splendid and idiosyncratic sense of humour must also be mentioned. To give one example from many, she once referred in a letter to someone who was 'now learning to stand on her own feet – which always sounds so unnecessarily uncomfortable'. Clive was perhaps uniquely fortunate in having married someone who had been prepared to help and support him with such instinctive loyalty and unselfishness in activities not all of which she could have found interesting or rewarding. And in spite of the collections that they assembled, and of Clive's important achievements both at home at Parham and in business all over the world, nobody would have been more surprised than Clive and Alicia that this account of their lives has been written.

APPENDIX A
The Library at Parham

The library at Parham is not what it may seem to the casual observer. A glance at a work of the Goupil series, a set of the Hakluyt Society, numerous early twentieth-century art reference books in lush morocco bindings commissioned by Bumpus, an extra-illustrated Nelson, *History of Islington*, 1811, side by side with an extra-illustrated Walpole *Letters*, might justifiably lead one to suppose that this was the archetypal 'gentleman's library' of the era. But the Nelson is no bookseller's compilation: brimming with added drawings, ballads, playbills, caricatures, and squibs, this is the copy owned and grangerised by George Daniel (1789–1864) of Canonbury Square. At the Daniel sale of 1864 it was bought by Henry Huth. The Walpole is rich in relevant engraved portraits and views; the bonus is the autograph letters by, *inter alios*, Addison, Burke, Chesterfield, Garrick, Hume, Johnson, Horace Mann (friend of Walpole), Mrs Piozzi, Pope, Scott, Sterne, Voltaire, and Walpole himself.

Plate books – aquatint or otherwise – abound. Loggan's *Oxford* and *Cambridge* are a matching pair in contemporary red morocco. A magnificent Kip *Britannia illustrata* in contemporary vellum gilt is flanked by Charles Montague, first Earl of Halifax's copy of Blaeu's *Tooneel der Steden Netherlanden*. Here too are Pine's *Tapestries*, Bentley's *Designs* for Gray, and two of the most famous French baroque books on horsemanship, Pluvinel's *L'Instruction du roy en l'exercice de monter à cheval* and *Le Cavalerice françois*. Inevitably there are the Ackermann *Microcosm* and Pyne *Royal Residences*; less predictable are the aquatint panoramas and peepshows, and the Lugars and Dearns which introduce a distinguished run of books on cottage architecture. If there are two copies of Nayler's *Coronation of George IV*, it is because one is on ordinary paper, the other on thick paper printed in gold. Likewise, there are multiple copies of Dickinson's *Great Exhibition*, one with plates tinted, another with plates coloured, a third in original parts, and a fourth with the plates in proof. Constable's *Various Subjects of Landscape*, 1833, is also a proof copy in wrappers.

Natural history is as rich botanically as it is ornithologically. Redouté's two masterpieces, *Les Roses* and *Les Liliacées*, rub shoulders with Levaillant's *Birds of Africa, Parrots* and *Birds of Paradise*. Together these represent the finest book illustration of Napoleonic France – and the innovation of colour printing; this technique of stipple engraving paved the way for the Victorian heyday of colour printing. Refreshingly there are no Goulds; the library's strength lies in an earlier age. For the eighteenth century there is the most sumptuous of all florilegia, Trew's *Hortus nitidissimis . . . superbiens floribus*, published in three volumes over a span of thirty-six years at Nuremberg, 1750–86. This is one of the few complete copies known, bound in contemporary red morocco for Duke Albert Casimir of Saxe-Teschen (1738–1822), founder of the Albertina in Vienna. For the seventeenth century there is the first edition of Besler's *Hortus Eystettensis* [Altdorf] 1613, the plates uncoloured and showing the quality of the engraved work to its best advantage; and for the sixteenth century, not only an early *Ortus sanitatis*, but one of the rarest and most charming books in the library, an Italian woodcut bestiary, *Libellus de natura animalium*, printed at Savona in 1534. This is the copy exhibited at the National Book League's 'The Italian Book' in 1947; no other copy outside Italy is recorded.

This is not to give the impression that the natural history is all high-spots collected by rote. Knip's *Les Pigeons* is a natural candidate for any great library, as are the works of Brookshaw, Catesby, Curtis, Edwards, Furber, Merian, Thornton, and Weinmann, to select only a few of the more obvious names that loom from the shelves. More eclectic is the inclusion of Barlow, Bonnant, Hollar, and Marmaduke Cradock (his spirited groups of birds engraved c. 1740 by Josephus Sympson – here coloured). And there are continual surprises. The Duhamel du Monceau *Traité des Arbres* is Madame de Pompadour's copy. Ferrari's *Hesperides*, Rome 1646, the first book devoted to citrus fruit, is a classic of baroque illustration almost always found plain; this is the exception, a coloured copy, in near-contemporary morocco for Baron Somers. And why some ten copies – a veritable flock – of Sweet's *British Warblers*, the visitor may ask? Because it was one of Alicia Pearson's personal favourites.

There are similar pleasures among the atlases and travel books. Saxton's *Atlas*, c. 1580, the first county atlas of England and Wales, has the maps coloured and heightened in gold; Blaeu's *Atlas major*, 11 vols., is no less splendid a copy in contemporary red morocco. One rich vein of travel lies in the exploring voyages round the world and to the South Seas. It begins with a set of Purchas' *Hakluytus Posthumus*, 5 vols., 1625; Tavernier's *Six Voyages* 1678, in a fine Restoration binding of morocco gilt; Narborough's *Voyages* 1694; a set of Dampier, 4 vols., 1697–99; and the Hacke *Collection of Voyages* 1699. It continues through the 18th century with Funnell's *Voyage round the World* 1707; Rogers' *Cruising Voyage* 1712; Shelvocke's *Voyage* and Captain Uring's *History*, both 1726; Betagh's *Voyage round the World* 1728; and a large paper copy of Anson, again in contemporary morocco. It concludes with a set of Captain Cook's three *Voyages*, which is in turn succeeded by two lavishly illustrated books to celebrate the Golden Age of Australia, James Wallis's *New South Wales* 1821 and Joseph Lycett's *Views of Australia* 1824–25 the last with an idyllic, tempting series of plates rendering the country more English than England. Similarly, three classic nineteenth-century folios devoted to Mexico – Dupaix, *Antiquités mexicaines*, Paris 1834; Nebel, *Viaje pittoresco de la*

Republica Mejicana, Paris 1839; and Waldeck's *Voyage pittoresque dans la Province d'Yucatan*, Paris 1838 – mark the emergence of an independent Mexico where fifty years or so later Lord Cowdray was to establish his own empire.

The most remarkable sequence of books in the library is the armorial bindings, some 450 volumes dating from the sixteenth to the early nineteenth century. The great majority are English, and the collection is richest in the sixteenth and seventeenth centuries. There is no comparable collection in private hands: its nearest rival is the Clements collection in the Victoria and Albert Museum. Here are books bound for Elizabeth I, James I, Prince Henry, Charles I, Anne of Denmark, Charles II, James II, William and Mary, Queen Anne, and the Old and Young Pretenders. And so too for many of the book-collecting public figures of Tudor and Stuart England, Thomas Wotton, Robert Dudley, Earl of Leicester, Lord Burghley, Sir Christopher Hatton, Sir Francis Walsingham, Sir Francis Bacon, Herbert of Cherbury, Sir Robert Cotton, Sir Robert Naunton, Archibishops Laud and Sancroft, Sir Kenelm Digby, and John Evelyn. One of the grandest volumes is the large paper copy of Bacon's *Instauratio Magna* 1620, first edition, first issue, in its original 'presentation binding' of limp vellum gilt, with Bacon's crest of a boar stamped on the sides. (An alternative version of the Bacon boar features on a copy of Strozzi, [*Poemata*] 1530.) Hardly less exceptional is a first edition (traditional 'sixth' title) of Milton's *Paradise Lost*, in contemporary red morocco with the arms of John Sheffield, Duke of Buckingham and Normanby (1648–1721). Chapman's *Homer* is in red morocco with the crest of Charles I; Descartes' *Principia philosophiae*, etc., 3 vols., Amsterdam 1644, in red morocco with the Strafford crest; Salusbury's *Mathematical Collections* (vol. 1 only, as usual) in red morocco for James Duke of York; and Burnet's *Theory of Earth*, 2 vols., 1684–90, a large paper copy in red morocco for Philip Stanhope, second Earl of Chesterfield (1633–1713). Two notable architectural titles are a folio Vitruvius, Venice 1567, again with the Strafford arms, and the first edition of Palladio, Venice 1570, Consul Smith's copy.

There are three bindings from the library of Wotton (1521–87), the English Grolier: Matthew of Westminster's *Flores historiarum* 1567 (Moss 120), a Boccaccio *De claris mulieribus* 1521 (apparently not in Moss), and the Estienne *Dictionarium historicum* 1561 (Moss 116). Robert Dudley, Earl of Leicester (1532–88), England's first great collector of bookbindings, is represented by another three bindings, the most interesting of which is an Italian Bible, Geneva 1562, which was a New Year's gift to him from an Italian diplomat in London. It was bound by the 'Morocco binder' (Nixon, no. 8), and is one of some fifteen books from Dudley's library to carry the 'secret signature' believed to connect him and Queen Elizabeth – a challenge for cryptographers. One of the smallest bindings in the collection is a 1604 *Imagines mortis* from the travelling library of Prince Henry, a striking physical contrast to the lavish folio Book of Common Prayer of 1616 bound for Charles when he succeeded his brother as Prince of Wales. Another binding for Charles Prince of Wales is the dedication copy of Casaubon's *Original of Idolatries*, 1624.

Royal taste continues to be exemplified in the French bindings, books bound for Marguerite de Valois, Louis XIII, Anne of Austria, Louis XIV, and Louis XV, many of whose portraits were also acquired for Parham. So, too, for Colbert and – much rarer – Nicolas Fouquet, the financier. One of several 'fanfare' bindings is a ten-volume Latin Bible, Paris 1652, (Old Testament only) from the Schiff collection, uniformly tooled *au pointillé* with a couped head in each of the corners and the added arms of Louis-Urbain Le Vèvre de Caumartin, Marquis de St. Ange (1653–1720), a great book collector. (In 1931 the New Testament volumes completing the edition belonged to M. L. Gruel.)

To accompany the bindings, and to make them more accessible, is an impressive holding of armorial reference books allied in turn to many sixteenth-, seventeenth- and eighteenth-century manuscript armorials. These range from the Shirley armorial of c. 1572 intended for presentation to Queen Elizabeth to something more bizarre, an 18th century MS handbook of arms which clearly served as a coachbuilder's pattern-book.

Other books in the library are as eclectic as they are fun. Of two copies of Holland's *Heroologia* [1620], the first English portrait book, one is a presentation copy, the other – the Britwell copy – belonged to Buchelius, the author of the commendatory verses beneath the portraits. From the Rolle Library is a sammelband of plays by Dryden and Davenant in a dazzling red morocco. And there are some interesting Blakes; an uncut *Night Thoughts*; a Thornton Virgil with the Blake woodcuts; Dante Gabriel Rossetti's copy in contemporary morocco of Malkin's *Father's memoirs* to which Blake contributed a frontispiece, and Salzmann's *Elements of Morality* 1791, translated by Mary Wollstonecraft with plates attributed to Blake. Smollett's *Plays*, 1777, is in a Scott of Edinburgh binding; Grahame's *Birds of Scotland and other Poems*, 1806, carries the signatures of the Ladies of Llangollen; and George Darley's lyrical drama *Sylvia*, admired by Coleridge and Mrs Browning, is a presentation copy in original boards to Maria Edgeworth.

A particular enthusiasm for Sir Joseph Banks is evidenced not only by the travel books but by several books from his library, his Somerville's *Chase* 1735, a Boswell *Life of Johnson* with an autograph letter addressed to him tipped in, and a Russian Catechism of 1713. A Hamilton's *Vesuvius* 1772 belonged to his only sister, Sarah Sophia Banks. But if there is one shelf (or cupboard) most closely associated with the house, it is surely that devoted to Robert Curzon. Here are the first (and later) editions of his two travel books, *A Visit to the Monasteries in the Levant* 1849, and *Armenia* 1854, and such rarer, less familiar works as his *Accounts of the More Celebrated Libraries in Italy* 1854, published by the Philobiblon Society, and *The Lay of the Purple Falcon* 1847, issued in an edition of only 30 copies. A counterfeit medieval ballad (begun by Bishop Heber), *The Lay* professes to be a translation of a manuscript at Parham. Here too are books from his library and a collection of autograph letters. But the triumph of the collection must be the presentation copy of the *Visit to the Monasteries of the Levant* which Curzon inscribed to his bride on their wedding-day.

NICHOLAS POOLE-WILSON

APPENDIX B

The speeches of Lord Rothermere and Lord Reith in the House of Lords debate on B.O.A.C. on 14 April 1943 indicate the strength of feeling of Clive's allies, who thought he was badly treated. Lord Sherwood, replying lamely for the Government, was not able to reveal the real reason for the necessity of air transport coming more fully under the control of the Air Ministry, which had to do with secret plans for the subsequent movements of airborne troops.

British Overseas Airways Corporation

VISCOUNT ROTHERMERE rose to call attention to the composition of the Board of the British Overseas Airways Corporation and to the civil aviation policy of the Ministry disclosed in the White Paper issued by the Secretary of State for Air; and to move for Papers. The noble Viscount said: My Lords, considerable anxiety has been caused by the changes which have taken place upon the Board of the British Overseas Airways Corporation, and I hope that to-day the noble Lord, Lord Sherwood, will be able to give us some further information which will help to restore confidence. The British Overseas Airways Corporation is not an institution which has gone on for very long; it is, of course, an amalgamation of the organizations of Imperial and British Airways, which were in existence before the war. When that amalgamation took place a very vast organization was in fact taken over. I believe that the number of men employed, or who were employed a short time ago, by the British Overseas Airways Corporation is in excess of 15,000. There is there the nucleus of an organization which we all hope will take a great part in post-war aviation.

At the present time we have a new policy laid down in the White Paper, which has to do with a new creation known as the Royal Air Force Transport Command. But before I come to that I should like to point out that this constitution of the British Overseas Airways Corporation, as it was originated, cannot possibly function unless it is given a great degree of independence. Nobody, when this was originally considered, imagined that British civil aviation could possibly be conducted by a Government Department. In order to avoid that, arrangements were made whereby a new kind of institution was set up which, although owned by the Government, was to be independent of the Government. The directors were to be appointed by the Government but, once appointed, they were to conduct the affairs of the organization. The only institution like it, I think, that had existed before was the B.B.C. That I believe was the model on which the constitution was more or less framed. But it will be apparent to your Lordships that it is extremely difficult to conduct any organization if it is to be continually interfered with by the Air Ministry, and I should like the noble Lord, Lord Sherwood, to make quite clear how far that interference has gone in the past, and how far it is intended to go in the future.

The war record of the British Overseas Airways Corporation has, so far as I understand it, been a very considerable one. With the aircraft at their disposal they have managed to keep going a great many routes, and I believe at the same time they have been of tremendous assistance to the R.A.F. in the repair depot that they have in the Western Desert. Therefore when we come to the policy as outlined in the White Paper there is nothing new, and can be nothing new, in the B.O.A.C. co-operating with the R.A.F. It must have been co-operating with the R.A.F. ever since the war started, and certainly could have done nothing else once the Secretary of State had invoked Section 32 of the Act, which gave him the power to take over control of the concern. Therefore when we received the White Paper containing the correspondence that took place between the Secretary of State and the late Chairman of British Overseas Airways Corporation, there seemed to many of us to be an incomplete story.

It seemed an extraordinary thing that the four directors, men of considerable distinction, men of considerable commercial experience and great experience in aviation, should take it upon themselves to resign owing to the fact that a Transport Command had been set up. It seemed very strange that this situation should have arisen when it was quite apparent that there must have been co-operation and collaboration going on ever since the war started. On reading between the lines it would seem that there must be considerably more in the mind of the Secretary of State than has so far been disclosed. The Transport Command is an entirely new organization set up for the war effort. I do not want to criticize its setting up; on the contrary, it should in my opinion have been set up a long time ago. I think it has very considerable functions to perform, and it is quite obvious that in the war as it develops it will take a much greater part. But at the same time it seems very difficult to imagine why it is necessary for the Transport Command to take over some of the routes of the British Overseas Airways Corporation.

I will come in a moment to the resignations and the new appointments. But before I do that I should like to point out to Lord Sherwood what occurred in the United States. There, as your Lordships know, civil aviation is run by private enterprise. At one moment the President of the United States decided that he would try to run some of those services with the American Air Force. As your Lordships know, this very quickly came to grief and the President had to call off the American Air Force and give back the aviation to the organization which previously ran it. When the war started he never made a mistake of that kind again. He appointed a General of the American Air Force, General George, I believe, who called a conference in Washington of the executives of the principal air lines of the United States. The result of that conference was that instead of taking over and running all the civil air lines, he took over the executives of the civil air lines, put them all into uniform and said, "Now you will go on and run your businesses in order to contribute towards the war effort." It seems to me that something of the same kind is in the mind of the Secretary of State. We only seem, I think, to have got the first part of it, and I want to know from Lord Sherwood whether sooner or later we shall not find the British Overseas Airways in uniform. Already it is stated in the White Paper that some of the crews of the aircraft are going to be in uniform and therefore there is no reason why that should not be extended.

The thing I am worried about is lest we do precisely the opposite of what was done in the United States. In the United States the civil air lines have absorbed the Army Transport Command: in this country I am frightened of the Army Transport Command absorbing civil aviation. I see a very serious situation arising from that, and quite an unnecessary one, because the R.A.F. have no experience in transport. They have done a very considerable job in ferrying bombers over from America, but in the actual business of running the regular routes of air transport they have no experience, they have no executives who have any experience of any sort. I am sure that Lord Sherwood would agree that when we are discussing this question of post-war aviation we have all of us a certain responsibility in realizing that we first of all have got to win the war. The effort has got to be made in the first place to contribute everything we can towards victory, without sacrificing plans for the war where that is unnecessary.

It seems to me that the best plan would have been if the British Overseas Airways Corporation, instead of being absorbed by the Transport Command, had been taken as the nucleus and had built itself up into a Transport Command with all its skilled organization and all its experience and knowledge of transport. I may be wrong, but I think that is really the key to the resignations. The late directors of British Overseas Airways saw perfectly well – naturally they had seen it coming for a long period, not like noble Lords who only read about it in the White Paper – that eventually they would be sitting in an office as directors of an organization which had ceased to exist, which had in fact been taken over by the Army Transport Command, leaving them not obviously responsible for anything. That would be a real ground for resignation. Why they have not stated publicly and properly the grounds on which they really resigned – because Mr. Pearson's letter is extremely short and hardly to the point unless you read between the lines – I do not know, except it may be from some misplaced idea of patriotism, a belief that you should not kick up a row in war-time, whereas in fact the only way you can ever get anything done is exactly the other way round. Mr. Pearson said in his letter: "The proposed arrangements, however, result in a situation which is indefinite for the Corporation and which does little to improve the difficult conditions in which the Corporation has operated throughout its existence."

That sentence can mean a great deal or it can mean nothing. I am inclined to think it means a great deal. We have a right to know from the Minister whether that is true.

These distinguished gentlemen in the aviation world having resigned, the Government were faced with the obvious necessity and duty of appointing new directors. It would have seemed to me an opportunity of finding men who were distinguished not only in the world of aviation but also in commerce and putting them on the board, not only for the reason that they were the best men to run the organization but also to restore confidence so that people would understand that the Government still looked upon the organization as a very important one. But what do we find? Who has been appointed? First of all there is Sir Harold Howitt. We were informed in another place yesterday that he is only a temporary appointment. He has been made Chairman. He is, of course, a member of the Air Council, and I believe his principal duties have been checking up on supplies. Why was he appointed even temporarily unless the intention originally was not to appoint him temporarily, and unless the original intention was to have him there so that he could be his master's voice?

Then there is the second appointment, which is that of Mr. Marchbank. What is Mr. Marchbank doing on the board? He has already been considered too old to deal with the railways. He has already been retired from his previous occupation. Yet he is appointed a director, in his second childhood, presumably, to try and assimilate the intricacies of the aeroplane. The third appointment we have to deal with is that of Mr. Simon Marks. What are his qualifications for going on the board? At least he is a man who has experience in commerce. He has experience as owner or manager of a large chain of cheap stores, but I cannot conceive what qualifications he has for going on the board of British Overseas Airways. I have no doubt that when his appointment was announced and he was put last on the list, he was put down because he was considered a piece of sugar to cover up the pill of the other two appointments. If that is the case it must have been a war-time ration. I suggest to the Minister that he should really hesitate before he appoints the fourth director – because there is another one to come. How he is going to find another one suitable to join this motley crew already there, I do not know. He is certainly going to have difficulty in finding anybody to join a board which has obviously no responsibilities and which cannot be said to be a responsible board for conducting the air transport of this country.

I would like to ask my noble friend another thing. In the correspondence which took place Mr. Runciman made a very generous offer to continue his duties until a new Director-General was appointed. No new Director-General has been appointed as far as I know, but Mr. Runciman has not been asked to do anything whatever by the new board. He has not seen the new board, nor has he done any work whatever in connexion with the new board, although the Secretary of State in his reply said how very pleased he was that Mr. Runciman was going to carry on till his successor was appointed. You have got on this board at present three new directors, none of whom knows anything whatever about civil aviation, and no Director-General or Managing Director or whatever he is called. They have made no attempt whatever to use the experience of either the ex-Director-General or any of the other directors who have gone off the board. We are thrown back on the obvious idea that the board is not expected very much longer to conduct the organization as we have known it, and that in the next development you will find an Air Marshal in charge of it. Very serious considerations are involved in this matter, and those who not only feel strongly about the war effort but also about post-war aviation should make their protest.

I would like to point out at the same time how the powers of this board have been taken away. Perhaps it was just as well they were taken away before the new directors were appointed. The White Paper refers to the relationship between the British Overseas Airways Corporation and the Royal Air Force, and in 3 (*a*) it states: "Negotiations with or in neutral countries or with Dominion, Colonial or other Governments for the provision of civil facilities, etc., will be conducted by the Civil Aviation Department of the Air Ministry (or by the Corporation in cases where questions of policy do not arise)."

I should very much like to know what that means. Does it mean that negotiations that may now be going on, for instance, with the Dominions will be carried out by the Air Ministry and not by the board of British Overseas Airways? Where exactly is the dividing line? Where the question of policy ends and where the question of carrying it out starts, I do not know. I presume the Air Ministry will lay down the policy and the board will carry it out. I should like to have a little light upon that point. I would point out to the Air Ministry that it will be too late after the war to make these arrangements with the Dominions.

I do not know whether my noble friend Lord Sherwood was here when the Leader of the House was speaking, but I should draw his attention to one sentence in the speech of the noble Viscount, Lord Cranborne. He said that in peace you must prepare for war and in the same way he said in war you must prepare for peace. That is an idea that has certainly not yet penetrated the Air Ministry. They have not the faintest idea of preparing for peace. I suggest that if that is the policy of His Majesty's Government in the great international matters which we have been discussing this afternoon, it certainly should be the policy of His Majesty's Government with regard to post-war air transport, because post-war air transport is an essential part of any international arrangements that are made for the future of the world. I think that the Government should, first of all, approach all the Dominions. Perhaps the noble Lord will be able to tell us that that has already occurred. I think arrangements should be made with these Dominions as quickly as possible as to the part, not that this country is going to play in post-war aviation, but that the whole Empire or Commonwealth of Nations, whichever term pleases different sections of the House, should take with us in civil air transport after the war. Once that is done it will be perfectly easy to have an arrangement with the United States of America, but until that is accomplished you cannot possibly get any arrangement with the United States of America. And unless it is accomplished, and accomplished long before the end of the war, you may find that some of the Dominions have entered into other arrangements. The Government will certainly be held to account if that should happen.

I hope I have not been too hard upon the Air Ministry in this matter, but really noble Lords know that the record of the Air Ministry in civil aviation has not been a very good one. So bad has it been that I have heard it said from those Benches again and again that air transport should be taken out of the hands of the Air Ministry and given to another Ministry, such as the Ministry of Transport. But I am not qualified in any way to talk on that subject. I think it is one the Air Ministry should very seriously consider because if Parliament is dissatisfied with the conduct of air transport by the Air Minister that Ministry, when the war is over, will certainly find it taken out of their hands. It is not a question purely of this present crisis in the organization. It goes back over a very long history and it will have to be shown that the Ministry holds its responsibilities very much higher in the future if it wishes to continue to keep civil aviation within its power. I appeal to the Minister to take this matter in hand; otherwise, whatever beautiful speeches may be made from these Benches about post-war policies, if you once have unbridled competition in air transport after the war it will be quite unncessary to talk about a League of Nations, it will be quite unncecessary to talk about any organizations for the maintenance of peace, because you will have already sown the seeds of another war.

LORD REITH: My Lords, may I give you some of the post-war history of the Corporation in order that you may perhaps have a more accurate picture of what has been taking place recently? And may I tell the noble Lord who has just spoken that in my opinion the formation of the Transport Command was by no means the sole but only the culminating reason for the resignations which a great many of us, certainly he and I, deplore? In July, 1938, the then Prime Minister asked me to leave the office where I had been happily occupied for a great many years and become Executive Chairman of Imperial Airways. I did as I was bid, with one condition.

Imperial Airways was then, as Lord Bennett mentioned recently, in considerable trouble which had led to the Cadman Report. That, as he said, was a scathing criticism of Government and Company. It criticized the general manager for taking too narrow and commercial a view of his responsibility without, I think, his having had an opportunity to answer the criticisms made against him. In any event, as Lord Morris remarked on the occasion of a recent debate in this House, he was in fact in charge of a commercial undertaking, and he and his directors regarded their first responsibility as being to shareholders. Few men have the same ideas about organization and administration, and Mr. Woods Humphery's ideas and mine were by no means akin, but much of the difference between his ideas and mine was due to the commercial régime under which he worked, and to his dividend obligations. No matter what any of us have thought about the constitution and the management of Imperial Airways, and whether or not they had been foresighted enough technically and politically, there is no doubt that they had a record of achievement under Mr. Woods Humphery of which any company in any country might well be proud; in some respects it was epic.

The condition to which I referred was that I should be supported in amalgamating Imperial and British Airways, and in turning the combination into a public service corporation. But, as I said on another occasion in your Lordships'

House, the serving of two masters is usually both morally undesirable and economically impossible. High dividend expectations from an essentially public service cannot be fulfilled without at least a risk of prejudice to the service and the public. But what justification had the noble Duke, the Duke of Sutherland, for saying in this House that more would have been done under a competitive system, and that when the British Airways came along to challenge Imperial Airways, the latter could not stand up to it and was swallowed up? I went to Imperial Airways with the intention of effecting the merger and the change of constitution. And perhaps Lord Strabolgi is convinced by this time that there are no private interests in the Corporation hampering, as he said, the future of civil aviation. He referred to the monopoly "so misused by the Corporation and its two predecessors." The Corporation has, in fact, never functioned at all, and has never been allowed to function.

I have ventured to tell your Lordships that I, more than any other, was responsible for what happened in the merging and the conversion of the two concerns. It took me a year to do. It might have taken some people longer. Obviously, I could not have done it without the support of the then Air Minister, Sir Kingsley Wood, who saw the business through despite opposition from members of his own Party. All through that troublesome year before the war we were arguing the clauses of the Statute – almost every line of it – but we were also looking forward – and this is what some noble Lords who have spoken in the debates recently do not seem to have realized – eagerly planning, trying hard to make people inside and outside the Government interested in civil aviation; routes in the Pacific, routes linking various parts of the Colonial Empire and the Dominions together; all sorts of plans, including something that the noble Lord has referred to this afternoon, the establishment of an Empire Corporation for which I had already secured the sympathy at least, and in some cases more than that, of several of the Dominions. In proof of that your Lordships will be interested to know that Sir Kingsley Wood had agreed in principle to keeping seats on the Corporation board open for representatives of the Dominions, so that an Empire Corporation was indeed thought of then. It would have been an immensely important experiment not only for civil aviation but for Empire relationships – British aircraft on full sail of wing flying the seven skies as once the ships of Britain sailed the seven seas. The embryo Corporation was prejudiced not just by lack of interest, but inevitably by war preoccupations, and by the difficulty of getting orders for new aircraft considered or existing orders delivered. Imperial Airways were badly off for machines, but we had little encouragement. Orders at home and in the United States were, on the outbreak of war, cancelled without it seemed any consideration for the part Air Transport should play even in war.

The noble Viscount, Lord Bennett, speaking in your Lordships' House recently, seemed to regard the Corporation as a satisfactory and reasonable instrument of Government purpose, but I regretted his suggestion that some members of the board had no right to be there because of their interests elsewhere. Mr. Clive Pearson is a director of the Southern Railway and Mr. Irvine Geddes is a director of the Orient Steam Navigation Company. I see nothing inconsistent in this, nor would other noble Lords who recommend that existing forms of transport should be associated with this new form – the Duke of Sutherland for instance, who recommended that civil aviation should be handed over entirely to shipowners. I suggest that Mr. Clive Pearson and Mr. Irvine Geddes deserve better than to have it said that their presence was not to the advantage of civil aviation.

I said the Corporation had never functioned. Constitutionally it was not established till after war broke out, and I have indicated how the pre-war year was occupied with the negotiations for its establishment, and how otherwise it was a year of frustration and disappointment. The moment it was established the Secretary of State for Air made an Order which brought it under his control. Its war-time duty is the maintenance of essential air-line communications, but it depends entirely on the Secretary of State for Air to enable it do to what he wants done. Air Ministry machinery and attitude to the Corporation have been unsatisfactory, and I say that the Corporation has never had a chance. The spokesman of the Air Ministry in another place made this statement: "Unless the Secretary of State considers that on grounds of public interest such a drastic step" – removal of directors – "is necessary, he will leave the management alone to carry on their own affairs."

I hope I may hear from the noble Lord this afternoon whether or not that is true. Has, in fact, the Secretary of State left the management alone "to carry on its own affairs"? I submit to your Lordships that the Corporation has not merely been controlled, as in war-time it should be controlled, in major policy, but also in executive detail, and that in everything but internal administration it has been under the close and often direct control of the Under-Secretary of State and the Director-General of Civil Aviation.

The Corporation directors appealed many times to the Air Ministry for the aircraft and personnel necessary to operate the routes which the Ministry wished operated. It was not always consulted in the allocation of aircraft and in some cases unsuitable planes were handed over to them. I ask the noble Lord if he is familiar with that, and if he can explain or excuse it. The Corporation has not been kept informed of technical development nor given the authority to obtain it. It has no official priority for spares or supplies. Its demands are routed through the Civil Aviation Department of the Ministry which is non-technical. It is not allowed to deal direct with the Royal Air Force, to whose requirements it has largely to operate. All negotiations have to be conducted through the Civil Aviation Department. As to personnel the Corporation, although an essential part of the war machine, is treated by and large as an ordinary commercial concern by the Ministry of Labour.

Members of the Corporation Board have only recently resigned after being for a long time so dissatisfied with the treatment they were receiving that they felt they could not carry on in such circumstances. As I have said, some of the conditions of the formation of this Transport Command were only the culmination of it. When Pan-American took over the Trans-African route they came complete with all essential stores, including radio and metereological equipment and even materials to construct living quarters. It was with chagrin that the Corporation compared its own treatment in similar circumstances from the Air Ministry. The attitude of the American Government and military authorities to their civil aviation operators is certainly in striking contrast to what we have here. When we were discussing the establishment of the Corporation one of the great advantages of the new system was that it would enable the Air Ministry to regard the Corporation, not with the suspicion often associated with a commercial concern, but, divested of dividend obligations and with the sole purpose of serving the public interest, as a trusted instrument of Government to which a great many of the functions previously exercised by the Civil Aviation Department would pass. What has in fact passed? There are many things which a Civil Aviation Department must for all time continue to do. But there are many things which even in war the Corporation should have done which it has never been allowed to do. A great deal of what the Civil Aviation Department has done is redundant and a retarding of war effort.

With a dozen old civil boats the Corporation has kept open the routes from Durban via Cairo to Calcutta and from West Africa to Cairo, nearly 30,000 miles long, twice a week. The only service in winter between the United Kingdom and Canada is operated by the Corporation, not by the Royal Air Force or the Americans, although the machines are American. It flew 10,000,000 miles in 1942; 21,500,000 capacity ton miles in 1942 compared with 12,500,000 in 1941 and 8,500,000 in 1940. Incidentally may I ask the noble Lord who will reply for the Ministry whether he happens to know what the Post Office thinks of the Air Mail performance, and whether the Post Office complaints are directed against the Corporation or the Ministry?

A further point on which I should like to have information is about advertising. The Corporation has not been permitted to advertise at all – not even a documentary film of its activities. Can we be told the reason for that? Is there some fear of alarming or offending any other country? The Corporation is a public body operating without profit as an instrument of the State. American commercial lines are encouraged to advertise their achievements. I think American air lines say quite openly that they are going to use the war to win the peace. The Vice-Chairman of the Civil Aeronautics Board, a Government official, said he was in favour – and he would not have said that unless he had public support behind him – of a national organization for civil aviation. And in America they do not usually favour national organizations. He said he was in favour of it – listen to this – "because no other basis would adequately reflect the fundamental policies which must be furthered." What are the fundamental policies which must be furthered – monopoly of air transport? If so, we are helping them to get it.

The position to-day is that, despite resounding declarations about bold measures, there has been no statement about Government policy and one imagines no policy to make a statement about. The Government attitude to the Corporation, to say the least of it, has been anomalous, if not rather shocking. Even yet transports are only to be planned on a trivial scale, and without them nobody, the R.A.F., the Corporation or the shipowners, can deliver the goods. We know that American transports will be better than ours for years to come – not because their manufacturers are better or cleverer but because they are practised. We know that the design and production of new aircraft is a matter of years. So in spite of anything that Lord Brabazon's Committee may have recommended or the Government adopted, we shall be in the hands of the Americans and dependent on them for a long time. As, by arrangement, we are making bombers and fighters and they transports, will they share as they should?

British Governments have not really cared for air transport; the Air Staff do not understand it, and it is not their job. I agree with what the noble Lord said about the Transport Command. It may be excellent in conception, but it is not the job of the Air Staff to run air transport. All the same, what would have happened had the Eighth Army had, say, 100 good transport planes to use? It might easily have meant that Rommel would have been caught before now. That is the burden of the complaint which I submit to your Lordships – that the Government made an instrument for civil aviation and then starved it. Will the noble Lord tell me what the Corporation has done to be treated in this way since it was established? The resignations of members of the directing body came as a shock, and it is shocking that things should have come to such a pass. Is there something radically wrong with the Corporation, and have they been given a chance to do better? If there is something wrong let us know of it. As things are now, owing to the way the Corporation has been treated it may well be beyond redemption.

Listen to this from the head of the operating company in one of the Dominions in a letter to me: "... We are most unhappy at the conspicuous absence of any British plan for the future, and the usual attitude of inertia – a point I have been striving to bring home as you will have seen by our *Gazette* and other literature I have sent you in recent months." And here is something from the editorial in an aviation paper published in that Dominion: "Our Empire air communications have ceased to exist ... one cannot call a few broken threads which finish in disconnected spots a line of Empire air communication in a true sense ... We all know about the plea of 'No aircraft.' Could not some have been bought, 'Lease-Lend,' or even have been scraped off the outer edge of bomber production at home? ... It will serve us right if, after we have won the war, we find we are not only not in the race of world air communications, but must stand in the sideline and wait to be told when we may tail along." It is not good, my Lords, that we should be written at like that. My noble friend Lord Rothermere is right – and I have information that gives point to it – when he stated that unless the Home Government can do something to convince people in the Dominions that they mean business in civil aviation, they will find the Dominions stretching out their hands to those whose hands are already stretched out to them.

Certain points of principle are clear. First, suppression of aviation in ex-enemy countries. Second, freedom of the air, that is to say no prohibition of flying over any country. Third – but this depends upon the answer to the fundamental question in the Report of Sir Francis Shelmerdine's Committee over a year ago – is there to be internationalization of operation or not? Some might well feel that the formation of a few large operating units working in international agreement had better come first – such as (*a*) United States and South America; (*b*) the British Commonwealth running the world Empire routes; (*c*) Russia; and (*d*) a European set-up in which England would be the predominant partner with subdivisions of each large group into geographical zones of operation for local traffic.

So there is my plea. Firstly, for a statement of national and international policy. Secondly, for the separation of civil aviation from the Air Ministry. Transport is transport and air transport is a form of it. Civil air transport, I submit, should be dissociated from bombing and fighting or moving air-borne troops, all of which are specialist military operations. It should in some way, I suggest, be linked with those other forms of transport which it will in part displace but with which it must co-operate if the public interest is to be properly served and the Empire have the place it should. Thirdly, that this Corporation, established as Lord Bennett said after a great deal of care – and nobody knows better than I how much care – should be given a chance to function. I see no reason to have more than one chosen instrument and many reasons against it. It is easy, out of prejudice or misconception, to dilate on the benefits of competition and the dangers of monopoly. There are neither dangers nor benefits that the Corporation, rightly circumstanced, rightly staffed and given the chance they have never had, cannot avoid or achieve. With scratch machinery, scratch personnel, and scratch machines they have done magnificently for the country. They ask to be given the chance to do what they were formed to do. What has been achieved by Mr. Leslie Runciman, to whom great credit is due – more credit than he has been given – and the Corporation staff is through individual effort and determination, despite immense handicaps and obstructions. But there is no reserve and little hope, and the personnel is now greatly discouraged.

Finally, it is urgently necessary in the interests of civil aviation that that civil aircraft should be designed, and some prototypes be produced. The Corporation should be given authority to do this. Presumably unless the Minister has something different to tell us to-day, post-war responsibility will be theirs. Unless these things are done and done quickly the British Empire will, in this respect, in the deplorable words of the Dominion commentator, be forced to "stand in the side lines and wait to be told if and when it may tail along."

THE JOINT PARLIAMENTARY UNDER-SECRETARY OF STATE FOR AIR (LORD SHERWOOD): My Lords, I should like at the outset to thank the noble Lord, Lord Rothermere, for giving me, before this debate began, an idea of the questions he was going to ask. As your Lordships realize, this question of civil aviation is a very important one. It covers not only the narrow question that is on the Paper, the question of B.O.A.C., but it also involves our relations after the war with the United Nations and our Dominions. I can take no exception to the spirit of the speech made by the noble Lord who moved this Motion. A very important decision was taken by the directors of the British Overseas Airways Corporation when they decided to resign, but I think it would be wrong to say, as has been represented I think by the noble Lord, Lord Reith, and perhaps by some other noble Lords, that something more than what was said by Mr. Clive Pearson in his letter to the Secretary of State was behind these resignations. I think there has been a certain amount of confusion in regard to this.

The noble Lord, Lord Rothermere, asked me if the decision was a sudden one or whether there had been disagreements over a long time. I can assure him it was a sudden decision. It came as a surprise to the Secretary of State. There is, incidentally, some misapprehension as to the position of the Air Council in this matter. It is the Secretary of State who is responsible for civil aviation not the Air Council and the board dealt with him and not the Air Council in trying to reach an agreement. The Secretary of State thought he was going to obtain it and it came as a complete surprise to him when the directors said they felt they could not accept the agreement in the form he suggested. I think if noble Lords will read the White Paper they will agree that the point on which disagreement arose is one on which it is absolutely essential, in war-time, for the Secretary of State to safeguard himself. At this point I would like to say that the B.O.A.C., as it is called for short, has done an immense amount of good work up to the present time and has achieved great things, especially in the Middle East, where it has been of immense assistance to the Royal Air Force. There is still a feeling which was expressed by at least one noble Lord that the position of the ex-directors was undermined by interference from the Air Ministry. That point was made particularly by Lord Reith, who said that there was constant interference and he implied that this was the main reason for the decision to resign. I can tell the noble Lord definitely that that was not so. There was no interference.

Under Section 32 of the Act the Corporation has been required by an Order to place B.O.A.C. at the Secretary of State's disposal during the war. The necessary control of war-time policy which arises under this Act has been carried out through directions issued by the Secretary of State through the medium of progress meetings under the Joint Under-Secretary of State, the right honourable Captain Balfour, but management has been left entirely to the Corporation. No orders affecting management were given at these progress meetings. The members of the Corporation were entirely responsible for management questions. I can assure the noble Lord, Lord Rothermere, and also the noble Lord, Lord Reith, who I wish was in his place because he made great play with this point, that there is no substance in the complaint that there was interference either by the Air Council – that is not possible – or at the progress meetings which merely dealt with questions of policy and had nothing to do with management.

The members of the Corporation – they have been called the board although there is no board really – resigned and, as I have said, this came as a surprise to the Secretary of State. What was the Secretary of State to do? It was his duty to find other people to carry on. He has found three new members of the Corporation who, I regret, have been very much criticized. In war-time eminent people do not stand waiting ready at hand to undertake important and responsible positions of this kind. The Secretary of State put in as Chairman Sir Harold Howitt. I would stress the fact, which has always been made clear by the Secretary of State, that Sir Harold Howitt's appointment is only temporary. Attacks have been made upon him because there appears to be an idea that he is simply a chartered accountant who knows nothing at all about aviation. Sir Harold Howitt, however, is a very distinguished gentleman who moreover has been a member of the Air Council since 1939. In the last war he won both the D.S.O. and the M.C. He is a man of great ability, a man who not only knows a great deal about aviation but who possesses great experience in business management.

Then there are the other members of the board. There was one gentleman who did not resign, Mr Gerard d'Erlanger. He has considerable knowledge of the air. At the moment he is controlling the Air Transport Auxiliary. There are two other members who have been criticized. One is Mr. Simon Marks. In this organization you must have people capable of running a large scale business and Mr. Simon Marks has had a remarkably successful business career. I am sure we shall not find him wanting. The other is Mr. Marchbank, who is very well known in trade union circles; a man who has the complete confidence of the trade unions. There are a large number of employees in this Corporation and you cannot leave personnel problems out of account. Those gentlemen form, I submit, a good board.

I do not wish to go into smaller points, but I have been asked how much is paid to Sir Harold Howitt. He is not paid as chairman of B.O.A.C., or for his services on the Air Council or for any of his other services to the State. I think it right to state this. As for this appointment of a permanent Chairman, I want to make clear as my right honourable friend has said in another place that the Secretary of State is not going to be hurried into finding a Chairman. This is a very important appointment, as noble Lords who have great knowledge have pointed out, and not one to be made quickly in order to settle with the Press or public. It is not easy to find the right person as Chairman of this Corporation and my right honourable friend must be given time in making the appointment. Another appointment, the importance of which cannot be stressed too highly, is that of Chief Executive, the post previously held by Mr. Leslie Runciman. That appointment has also not yet been made. The appointment will, however, not be made by my right honourable friend but by the members of the Corporation. They will not only appoint him, but they will also decide upon his salary. He is their servant. His appointment has nothing to do with the Secretary of State. It would be wrong to make this appointment in a hurry too. A quick appointment would not necessarily be the right one. At the present moment management is being carried on by an Executive Group at Bristol, and they report daily as a body to Sir Harold Howitt. That is how the executive work has often been carried on before in the absence of the chief Executive.

There are some awkward questions worrying everyone as to how far Air Transport Command will absorb the activities of B.O.A.C. It is not intended that Air Transport Command should absorb those activities. We wish to avoid duplication and to find some way by which we can get the closest collaboration between the two organizations. Not only will the Corporation remain as it is, however, but it will grow bigger. I am not going to quarrel, although it would be easy to do so, with noble Lords who said that in peace-time we should prepare for war and in war-time prepare for peace. Like all quack remarks that is a mere half-truth. In war-time you have to get peace before you can prepare for it although I agree that peace must be kept in sight. A great many of the criticisms which have been made arise because we have had to put so much energy and must continue to put all our energy into the war efforts of the country. It is quite right that noble Lords should ask what our views are about what is going to happen after the war, and whether Transport Command will operate services after the war. On this point I have no doubt that for many months after the close of the war the Command will continue manifold ferrying tasks, and it seems likely that it will continue to operate services if only for a time. Indeed it may be part of the post-war policy of the Royal Air Force to keep an Air Transport Command in being as a military instrument.

Another question that has been asked is: "Will the Secretary of State hand back to the Corporation the powers that he has taken under Section 32 of the British Overseas Airways Corporation Act at the end of the war." Of course it would be logical to suppose that after the emergency which led the Secretary of State to take this action has passed away, the Secretary of State would hand back the powers he has assumed, unless Parliament in its wisdom has meanwhile legislated otherwise. In any case the validity of the action taken under Section 32 does not extend beyond a "time of war, whether actual or imminent or of great national emergency." As I say, it seems natural and logical therefore that these powers should lapse at the end of the war.

Now I come to the big questions which have been raised with regard to the Dominions and Colonies and the United States. These questions are of the highest importance. I do not see my noble friend Viscount Bennett here now, but I know that there are several of your Lordships who take the greatest interest in these very important matters. I can assure your Lordships that the Secretary of State fully realizes the importance of exploratory discussions with the Dominions on civil aviation. In fact such discussions are now taking place. I will not weary noble Lords by reading the speech of my right honourable friend, Sir Archibald Sinclair, in another place, but in his statement on the air estimates he did make it quite clear that this action was being taken. I cannot give you any account of the course of these discussions and indeed it is for the Dominion Governments to state their own policy. I do think, however, that it might be well to draw your Lordships' attention to the statement which was made by the Prime Minister of Canada in the Canadian House of Commons on April 2nd. It shows, I think, not only that discussions have been taking place but also that they are bearing fruit.

Mr. Mackenzie King, whose words, I think, are of the greatest importance, said: "The Canadian Government strongly favours a policy of international collaboration and co-operation in air transport, and is prepared to support in international negotiations whatever international air transport policy can be demonstrated as being best calculated to serve not only the immediate national interests of Canada but also our over-riding interest in the establishment of an international order which will prevent the outbreak of another world war." That is going a long way. There is no doubt that the Dominions are thinking on bigger lines than those merely of domestic policy. There is also no doubt that when these discussions with the Dominions and Colonies have resulted in a measure of agreement, it will be of the highest importance to open discussions on these questions with America. I do not think noble Lords would expect me to go further than that. Obviously it is better to wait until agreement has been reached with the Dominions and the Colonies before opening discussions with America on these very big questions of post-war policy.

I was asked whether we were going to restart certain services between India and Australia. I think it will be obvious that for reasons connected with national security I cannot go deeply into that. To do so would obviously reveal information which might be useful to our enemies. I was also asked whether existing B.O.A.C. routes are being cut down. Noble Lords are quite right to ask these questions. The answer to this particular question is that the routes to be operated by the Corporation and Transport Command respectively have not been finally determined. They may, of course, vary from time to time. It may be expedient to transfer the operation of some routes from the Corporation to the Royal Air Force, and the reverse may also apply. But if we take over – and by "we" I mean the Royal Air Force – any of the routes which are now operated by the Corporation, it will in no way reflect on the capabilities of the Corporation or of their staff and their pilots, for whose courage and efficiency we have nothing but the highest praise. It would merely be because of necessity arising from war operations that a route might have to be taken over.

Now comes the big and troublesome question which is almost bound to come up whenever you have discussions on civil aviation: Are we going to retain B.O.A.C., as the "chosen instrument", for civil air transport, after the war? Lord Reith, who was one of the founders of the organization, touched on this particular question. I wish that my noble friend, Lord Reith, was here now, because he would no doubt answer my noble friend Lord Milford on this point. Obviously it was to him and not to me that Lord Milford directed some of his remarks. Now the question whether the method of the single chosen instrument is the best method of conducting air transport after the war is one of the major issues of policy on which His Majesty's Government is not, and cannot, yet, be in a position to reach a final conclusion. Obviously it is to some extent bound up with the question of the form and extent of international or inter-Dominion collaboration after the war on which discussions are now proceeding with the Dominions and India, and will, in due course, be extended to cover a wider field. Meanwhile, the Government must retain their freedom of action, and avoid unilateral declarations of policy which would circumscribe or prejudge those discussions in any important respect. I think it must be clear to your Lordships that that should be the policy of His Majesty's Government at the present time. We all would like definite answers and solutions, but it is impossible to arrive at the final shape of post-war civil aviation at this stage of the war.

I should like, finally, to thank the noble Viscount for the way in which he brought this matter before us. We did not wish this board to resign, and there was no sinister, underlying motive in their resignation; but, the members having resigned, it was the duty of my right honourable friend the Secretary of State to appoint a board and to see that the organization is carried on. That he has done and will continue to do. I hope that the noble Viscount will be satisfied.

VISCOUNT ROTHERMERE: My Lords, I should like to thank the noble Lord, Lord Sherwood, for his very informative speech. I think that he has reassured us on a number of points. The resignations are still somewhat inexplicable, but we must accept his explanation. With regard to Dominion policy, I can only express the hope that, in approaching the Dominions, the Government are not being as vague as they are in their explanations to this House. I hope, too, that they are not being as vague as the quotation which Lord Sherwood made from Mr. Mackenzie King's speech. I trust that we are getting a little beyond all that verbiage, and are going to get down to some sensible arrangement. Apart from those comments, I thank the noble Lord very much indeed, and I beg leave to withdraw my Motion.

Motion for Papers, by leave, withdrawn.

Index

Abbey, Major Jack, 126
Aberdeen, 94, 95
Aberdeen Free Press, 44
Acton Bolt Co., 70
Admiralty, 24, 25, 26, 27, 51, 52, 60
Admiralty Harbour (Dover), 11, 14, 19
Adventures, 83
Aeronautics, 98
Agnew, Thos. and Sons, 81
Air Board, 51
aircraft companies, 92–106
Aircraft Production, Ministry of, 98, 100, 102
aircraft types, 93, 99, 100, 102
Airlie Gardens (No. 16), 13
Air Ministry, 98, 100, 103, 106
Air Transport Auxiliary Command, 100
Air Transport Command, 105, 106
Albury Park, 127
Aldeburgh, 78
Alessandri, President Arturo, 59, 64
Allende, President Salvador, 63
Alvarada railway, 23
Amberley, 40
Amerada Company, 66, 67
American Companies, 56, 64, 66, 72
American and Foreign Power Co., 64
Anglo-Mexican Petroleum Products, 23, 24, 25, 28
Anglo-Persian Oil Co., 30, 65
Anne, Queen of Austria, 81
Anne, Queen of Bohemia, 86
Anne, Queen of Denmark, 85
Aquila Oil Co., 22, 66
armorial stamps (on books), 88–9, 90
Arts Council, 117

Arundel, 33
Ashburnham, Lady Catherine, 128
Ashburnham Place, 86
Ashland Oil Co., 68
asphalt, 25
Assheton family, 86
Athens, 57, 102
Athens – Piraeus Electricity Co., 69–70, 118
Athens – Piraeus Railway, 70
'Aunt Arab' (Mrs Charles Camm), 42, 110
Australia, 29, 78, 100

Babington, 86
Baden-Powell, General Robert (Lord), 18
Balcombe House, 29, 30, 33, 34
Balfour, Captain Harold, MP, 93, 94, 99–100, 103, 106
Balmaceda, Prime Minister José Manuel, 59, 61
Baltimore – Ohio Railway, 56
Banks, Sir Joseph, 38, 80, 83, 84, 87, 90
barrage balloons, 107
Batemans, 127
Battenberg, Princess Louise of (Queen of Sweden), 75
Beaufort, Duke of, 78, 84
Beaverbrook, Lord, 100, 101
Beckford, Alderman, 81
Beggar's Opera, The, 84
Belgium, 95
Bellotto, Bernardo, 83
Bembridge, 79, 109
Berlin, 95, 96
Blackpool, 94

151

Blackwall Tunnel, 11
Blickling Hall, 34
Bloomfield, Thomas, 70
Blunt, Wilfrid Scawen, 126
BOAC (British Overseas Aircraft Corporation), 12, 92, 97–106, 107, 110, 118
Board of Trade, 97
Body, T. B., 23, 30, 66, 111
Boeing 314A flying-boats, 100
book-collecting, 88–91, 94, 130–4
Boston House, 82
Bournemouth, 93
Bouvier, Mr, 67
Bowhill, Air Chief Marshal Sir Frederick, 105
Bowring, C. T. & Co., 20, 27
Brabourne, arms, 39: Dowager Lady, 29, 119, 120; Lord, 28, 90
Bradford, Lord Mayor of, 11, 17
Braganza, Princess Catherine of, 82
Brandon, Charles, Duke of Suffolk, 86
Brighton, 92
Bristol, 107
British Airways, 94, 95, 103, 104, 110
British Continental Airways, 95
British Council, 108
Brodies (agents), 43, 44
Brown, Harold, 106
Brussels, 71, 95
Budapest, 95
Buena Vista, River, 22
Buenos Aires, 58, 62, 94
Burdett-Coutts family, 82
Burmah Oil Company, 30, 65
Burnett, Frances Hodgson, 75
Burney, Fanny, 83
Burrell, Judy, 113
Burton Agnes, 119
Butler, R. A., 108
Bysshopp, Sir Cecil, 81; family, 39, 86; Sir Thomas, 37

Cadnam Report, 96
Cairo, 101
Cambridge University, 17, 26, 30, 125
Camco, 67

Camm, Mrs Charles ('Aunt Arab'), 110
Campbelltown, 95
Canada, 65, 67
Canadian Army, 113, 116
Canterbury, 25
Cardenas, President Lazaro, 71, 72, 73
Carlisle, 94
Carlsbad, 43
Carr, Mr, 66, 67, 68
Carroll, Lewis, 75
Carlton House Terrace (No. 16), 13
Cass, Annie (grandmother, 1st Lady Cowdray), 11, 12, 13, 16, 81; Sir John, 11, 80
Cass, B. C., 14
Castle Howard, 117, 127
Cecil, William, Lord Burghley, 85
cement works, 14
Central Bank of Chile, 55
Chamberlain, Sir Austen, 60
Chamberlain, Neville, 95
Chanctonbury Rural District Council, 41
Channel Islands, 93
Charles I, King, 84, 85, 86
Charles II, King, 86
Charles Edward, Prince, 86
Charles Street (No. 49), 29
Charlotte, Queen, 83
Chastleton House, 119
Chatsworth, 66
Chichester, 78
Chihuahua, 22
Chile, 28, 51–64, 69, 74, 92
Chilean Electric Tramway and Light Company, 53, 56, 58–9
China, 65; railways in, 14
cholera, 55
Christie's, 84
Churchill, Sir Winston, 100
Clacton, 94
Clark, Kenneth (Lord), 114
Claro, Don Samuel, 58–9, 61
Cleveland, Duchess of, 86
Colchester, 18; oyster feast, 18
Cologne, 95

Compania Chilena de Electricidad ('Chilena'), 54, 55, 56, 64
Compania Nacional de Fuerza Electrica, 56, 63
compensation, for oil fire, 22; for oil companies, 72–3
Cook, Captain James, RN, 81, 83
Copenhagen, 94
Cordoba, 23, 53
Cornforth, John, 46, 117, 119
Cornwall, 14
Country Life, 37, 46, 117
Courcier, Rosemary, 42, 129
Cowdray, Viscount, *see* Pearson
Cowdray Hospital Association, 35
Cowdray Hunt, 36
Cowdray Park, 17, 24, 25, 34
Cowdray Trust, 77, 118
Crabbet, 125
Credit Anstalt, 70
Cridland, Mr (butler), 26, 76, 77, 94
Croydon, 93
Cuba, 23
Curzon, Lord, 13, 28, 90, 119

Damaskinos, Archbishop, 108
Darnley, Lord, 82
Davies, Bill, 111
Davies, Gordon, 119
DC3 aircraft, 102
Delaware, 66
Del Rio, Mr, 61
Denman, Lady (sister), 29, 33. See also Pearson, Gertrude
Dering, Elizabeth, 81; Mary, 82
Deruet, Claude, 87
Deterding, Sir Henri, 52
Deutsche Petroleum Co., 25
Devereux, Robert, Earl of Essex, 84, 85
Devis, Arthur, 82
Devon, 68
Devonshire, Duke of, 13
DH86 aircraft, 93
Diaz, President Porfirio, 13, 17, 23, 24, 51, 71, 72; Carmen, 17; Porfirio (son), 22

Dictionary of English Sculptors, 117
Dillon, Read & Co., 66
docks, *see* harbours
Dolphin, 83
Dos Bocas oil well, 21
Dover, 11, 14
drainage, 14
Dring, Mr, 90
Dublin, 14
Dudley, Lord Henry, 84
Dudley, Robert, Earl of Leicester, 85
Dunecht, 12, 42, 44, 46, 47, 56
Dunstan, Saint, 36
Duran, Carlos Pinto, 58
Durham, 14
Dutch Government in Exile, 108
Duveen, Joseph (Lord), 87

Eagle Oil Transport Co., 24, 28
East Knoyle, 84
East London Waterworks, 14
East River tunnels, 11, 12
Eastbourne, 16
Eden, Anthony (Lord Avon), 108, 119
Edward VI, King, 84, 85
Edwards, Alfred, MP, 104
Edwards, Don Agostin, 59
Egypt, 65, 100
Electric Bond and Share Company, 60, 62
electricity, 23, 53, 54, 58, 64, 69, 92, 118. *See also* hydro-electricity
Elizabeth I, Queen, 81, 84, 85
Elizabeth, Queen of Bohemia, 84
Elizabeth, Queen Mother, 46
El Mercurio, 59
Elveden, Lord, 128
Empire Mail Scheme, 99
Endeavour, 81, 83
Erlanger, Gerard d', 100, 106; Leo d', 93, 102
Erlangers Bank, 94, 96
Erskine, Lady Isabella, 81
Ertz, Susan, 110
evacuees, 109–13
Exeter, 92
exploration, books on, 90

expropriation, (of Mexican Eagle Oil Co.), 24, 71, 72–3

farming, 125
Fawcett, John, 38, 84
Feilding, Lord, 84
Financial Times, The, 116
Fitzwilliam, Earl, 124
Fitzwilliam, Toby, 19, 38, 77, 123–4; Mrs Toby, 114
Foreign Office, 54, 57, 60, 64, 114
France, 65
Frankfurt, 95
Frankland, Sir Frederick, 32, 34, 35
Fraser, Andrew (Lord), 45; Mrs Frederick Mackenzie, 43, 44–5, 48; Michael, 45; Thomas, 45
Furbero oilfield, 22
Fuerza Motrices del Valle de Lecrin, 69
Furneaux, Captain, RN, 83

Gainsborough, Thomas, 80, 82, 84
Garrick, David, 82
Gatwick, 95
GEC (General Electric Company), 57
Geddes, Irvine, 104
Germany, 74
George III, King, 83
George IV, King, 90
George V, King, 46, 110
Georgian Group, The, 33
Gheeraerdts, Gerrard, 84
Gibson, Patrick (Lord), (son-in-law), 76, 116, 119; Lady, *see* Pearson, Dione
GKN (Guest, Keen & Nettlefold), 70
Glasgow, 94, 95
Gloucestershire, 14
Godfrey-Faussett, Captain Sir Bryan, RN, 110; Lady, 112
Godolphin Barb (Arab horse), 82
de Golyer, Mr, 66, 67, 68
Gonzalez (painter), 84
Gooden & Fox, Messrs, 82
Gouge, Sir Arthur, 93
Graham, Harry, 75
Granta, 16, 18, 20

Great Northern and City Railway, 14
Great Western Railway, 14, 93
Greece, 92
Greeks (in wartime London), 70
'Greek House', 108
Greville, Lord, 90; Mrs Rupert, 85, 117–18
Grove, Colonel Marmaduque, 63
Grosvenor family, 86
Grosvenor Square (No. 32), 30, 39, 55, 70, 74, 76, 77, 79, 80, 83, 107–9
Gunnis, Rupert, 85, 117–18
Gurdon, Robin, 73–4

Halifax (Nova Scotia), 11
Hamilton, Lady (Emma), 83, 123
Hanover, 94, 95
Hansard, 106
Harington, Lord, 84
harbours, 11, 12, 14, 16, 51, 64
Harding-Newman, Major, 34, 35, 40
Harlow, G. H., 84
Harriman, Averell, 101
Hartington, Lord and Lady, 66
Hatfield House, 127
Hay, G., 14
Heal, Victor, 39, 57, 62, 77
Henriette, Duchess of Orleans, 86
Henry IV, King of France, 81
Henry Frederick, Prince of Wales, 85
Hestia, 70
Heston, 95, 96
Highland Airways, 95
Highland Division, 49
Hillman Airways, 94, 103
Hind (yacht), 78
Hippodrome Theatre (New York), 56
Hogarth, William, 82
Hohler, Sir Thomas, 21
Holbein, Hans, 81, 87
Holland, 95
Hollywood, 94
Hondecoete, Gillis, 81
Hopkinson, F. T., 14
Hoppner, John, 81
Hopwood, Sir Francis, 26
House of Commons, 95
Howard, George, 117

Howard, Henry, Earl of Surrey, 84
Hugessen, Dorothea, 80; Mary, 80
Hughes-Stanton, Sir Herbert, RA, 84
hunting, 36, 78
Huntingdon Harford Library, 81
Hussey, Christopher, 37
Hyde, Anne, Duchess of York, 86
hydro-electricity, 51, 54, 70

Ibañez, President Carlos, 57, 58, 64
Imperial Airways, 12, 96, 97, 98, 99, 103
India, 100
India Office, 65
Infanta Maria Anna, 84
Inverness, 95
Iraq, 65, 101
Islay, 95
Isle of Man, 95
Italy, 105

James I, King, 85, 86
James II, King of Scotland, 45
James, William, 38
Jersey, 92
Jersey and Guernsey Airways, 93
Joad, Professor C. E. M., 40
John Edwards (yacht), 78
Johnson, Cornelis, 82
Johnson, Dr Samuel, 83
Juan Fernandez Island, 58
Just So Stories, 75
Jutland, Battle of, 19

Kansas, 66
Kelly, Dr William, 47–8
Kemp, Leslie, 70, 102
Kemp's Engineering Handbook, 23
Kenmay Church, 49
Kentucky, 68
kerosene, 25, 27
Kilmuir, Lord, 124
Kindersley, Lord, 54, 71
King's Lynn, 11
Kirk, Madame, 81
Knatchbull, Sir Edward, 80; family, 86; Joan, 80; Major Norton, 80; Sir Thomas, 82

Knatchbull-Hugessen, Alicia Dorothea, (wife), 31, 32, 35, 45, 46, 57, 59, 79; collects books, 88–91; in Chile, 62; death, 128; supports Greeks, 108–9; home life, 74–6, 114–15; marriage and children, 28–31; opens Parham to public, 117–23; remodels Parham, 39–40, 119; collects pictures, 80–8; and war evacuees, 109–13
Kneller, Godfrery, 81, 82
Knepp Castle, 113
Knole, 34

Lady, The, 29
La Florida Falls, 54
Lang, Andrew, 75
Largillière, Nicolas de, 86
Lazard Bros. & Co., 54–5, 70–1, 92, 118
Lear, Edward, 75
Leconfield, Lord, 36
Leeds, Dukes of, 82
Legranez, Marquesa de, 81
Lely, Sir Peter, 82, 86
Library (at Parham), Appendix on, 130–4. *See also* books, Parham
lighting, 56, 61
Lisbon, 102
Lloyd-George, Earl, 52
London, 92, 94, 96, 107
Longhi, A., 86
Loraine, Sir Percy, 108
Lorimer, Sir Robert, 46–7
Los Angeles, 94
Louis XIII, King of France, 81
Ludendorff, Field-Marshal Erich von, 28
Lutyens, Sir Edwin, 57

McCrindle, Major Ronald, 103, 110
MacDonald, K., 14
McQueen, Miss, 110,
Maggie (maid), 111
Maggs Bros. 128
Maipo, River, 54
Maitenes, 54, 56

Major, John, 82
Malmö, 94
Malta, 103
Mar, Earldom of, 25
Marlborough, Duke of, 17, 19
Marshall, Alan, 48
Mary, Queen, 46
Mary of Modena, Queen, 86
Mary Tudor, Queen, 87
Maxwell, Robert, 102
Mayer, M. André, 71
Meaning of Money, The, 23
Member for Mexico, 11
Men of War Becalmed, 84
Messel, Oliver, 119
Meštrović, Ivan, 119
Mexican Eagle Oil Co., 22, 23, 24, 51, 52–3, 65, 66, 71, 72, 92
Mexican Electric and Power, 55
Mexico, 11, 12, 14, 17, 20–5, 26, 41, 51, 54, 90
Mexico City, 11, 22, 23, 111
Midhurst Oil Co., 67
Mignard, Pierre, 86
Minatitlan oil refinery, 20
Moir, Sir Ernest, 64
Monckton, Sir Walter (Lord), 124
monks, 125
Monmouth, Earl of, 84
Montacute House, 34
More, Sir Thomas, 81
Morecambe, 94
Morocco, 65
Muir, Mrs, 81
Munich, 95
Murillo, Bartolomé, 81
Murray of Elibank, Lord, 65
Murray, Professor Gilbert, 108
Museum of the Army (Santiago), 63
Mytens, Daniel, 86

National Gallery, 114
National Portrait Gallery, 80
National Trust, 34, 117
National Trust for Scotland, 44, 86
nationalisation, 57

natural history, books on, 89–90
Newcastle-on-Tyne Electric Supply Ltd., 55
New York, 11, 12, 56, 94
Nice Clean Plate, A, 74
Nippy (yacht), 78
Nollekens, Joseph, 117
Normandy, 17, 33, 105
Northcliffe, Lord, 13, 52
Northumberland, Duchess of, 127
Northwick Park, 87

Odlum, Mr, 62, 63
oil, 51, 67, 91; Anglo-Mexican companies, 12, 22; discoveries, 20, 22, 66; German shortage of, 28; markets for, 23, 51; output, 66; refineries, 20; retailing, 21; wells on fire, 21, 22. *See also* Admiralty
Oklahoma, 66
Old Pretender, 86
Olivier, Herbert, 30
Omai (Tahitan chief), 83–4, 87
Orde, Alan Campbell, 96–7, 104
Orient Steam Navigation Company, 104
Orizaba, 23, 53
Orkney, 95
Orleans, Duke of, 86
Oxford University, 90

Paddockhurst, 13, 17, 24, 39, 77, 81, 82, 83, 88, 111, 125
Palestine, 101
Palairet, Sir Michael, 108
Palmer family, 37
panoramic rolls, 90
Parham, 12, 16, 26, 29, 30, 45, 46, 49, 57, 59, 62, 63, 74, 94; books at, 88–90, 130–4; open to public, 116–23; pictures at 80–8; purchase and alterations, 32–42; social life, 79; staff, 77–8; in war, 108–15
Parham in Sussex, 19
Paris, 24, 28, 94, 96
Parry, William, 87
Pawson, David, 70
Peake, Robert, 85

Pearson, Alicia Dorothea (wife), see Knatchbull-Hugessen; Annie (mother, 1st Lady Cowdray, GBE), see Cass; Angela (cousin, Hon. Mrs Robert Campbell-Preston) 29; Beryl (aunt), see Spencer-Churchill; Clive, aircraft interests, 92–106; early background and education, 11–19; birth, 13; at Cambridge, 16, 17–18; character, 76–7; business in Chile, 51–64; death, 128; helps Toby Fitzwilliam, 123–4; honoured by Chilean Government, 64; marriage, 29; Mechanical Sciences degree, 18; in Mexico, 17, 20–5; opens Parham to visitors, 116–23; on Pearson board, 30; retires, 127; at school, 16–17; tree-planting, 49; Dione (daughter, Lady Gibson), 30, 76, 78, 113–14, 116, 126; Geoffrey (brother, 27; Gertrude (sister, Lady Denman, GBE), 16, 18, 29, 44, 78; Harold (brother, 2nd Viscount Cowdray), 17, 25, 26, 35, 44, 78, 87; John (nephew, 3rd Viscount Cowdray), 29, 64, 105, 111, 116; Judith (niece, 'Judy', Lady Burrell, OBE), 78; Lavinia (daughter, Mrs Michael Smiley), 30, 47, 49, 74, 78, 79, 83, 94, 112, 114, 117, 128; Veronica (daughter, Mrs Patrick Tritton), 29, 74, 76, 78, 82, 83, 90, 93, 94, 109, 110–13, 116, 117, 118, 123, 125, 128; Weetman (1st Viscount Cowdray), 11–15, 26, 30, 51, 63, 80; in America, 17; created baronet, 13; buys Dunecht, 42, 43; electricity and trams in Chile, 54–5; MP for Colchester, 18; notes on firm's work, 14–15; oil business in Mexico, 20–5; in USA, 67–8; relations with Tonkin, 55–8; wealth, 32; Yoskyl (niece, Lady McCorquodale), 73

Pearson, Ernest, 64

Pearson, S. & Son, contractors (later Pearson Group), 11, 13, 14–15, 23, 24, 30, 35, 51, 52, 67, 71, 79, 92, 96, 102, 108, 116, 118, 127

Pedragal oil well, 20
Perkins, D. L., 108
Peru, 74
Peto, Sir Samuel Morton, 13
Petre, Mr (chauffeur), 76
Petworth House, 114
Phillips, Charlie, 110; 'Trix', 110, 111
Phipps, Captain Charles, RN, 84
pictures, 80–8
Pierce, Henry Clay, 20, 24
Pinochet, President Augusto, 63
polo, 17, 18, 25, 78
Poole, Oliver, 118
Portsmouth, Duchess of, 86
Port Talbot Docks, 14
Potrero oilfield, 22, 23, 30
Pourbus, Frans, 81
Poussin, Nicolas, 181
Prestwick, 107
Progress Petroleum Company, 67
Puebla, 23
Puebla Tramway, Light and Power Company, 51
Pulborough, 33

Quaritch, Messrs, 90, 128
quarries, 14
Quiller, John, 82, 128

Raeburn, Sir Henry, RA, 81
Railway Air Services, 93
railways, 11, 12, 14, 23, 56, 70
Ramsgate, 94
Red House, 78
Reed, C., 43
refineries, 20, 21
Reith, Sir John (Lord), 96, 97, 98, 99, 102, 106
Reynolds, Sir Joshua, RA, 80, 82, 83
Richmond, Duke of, 36
riding, 78. *See also* hunting, polo
roads, 28
Robbery under Law, 73
Robins, Rev. John, 17
Rolls-Royce cars, 42, 75, 110
Romney, George, 81, 82, 83

157

Roosevelt, President Franklin D., 72
Roper-Lumley-Holland, Mrs, 84
Ross and Wicklow Railway, 14
Rosse, Lord, 33
Roth, William, 84
Rothermere, Lord, 106
Rothschild family, 70
Rowse, A. L., 115
Royal Air Force, 97, 98, 99, 100, 102, 107
Royal Dutch Shell Oil Company, 24, 52, 53, 65, 73, 92
Royal Flying Corps, 92, 93
Royal Forestry Society, 126
Royal Philosophers' Club, 83
Royal Society, 81
Rugby School, 16–17
Rueff, Marcus, 112
Rufford Abbey, 84
Runciman, Leslie, 93, 97, 98, 99, 100, 103–4, 106, 110
Rycade Company, 66, 67
Ryder, Mr, 66, 67, 68
Rysbrack, J. Michael, 117

Sackville-West, Vita, 75
San Antonio, 94
St Christopher's School, 16
San Cristobal oilfield, 21
San Diego oilfield, 21
sailing, 29, 78–9, 97
Sandwich, Lord, 83, 84
Santiago, 54, 56, 57, 58, 61, 62
Saunders-Roe Company, 93
Savile, Lord, 84
schools, 16, 30, 75, 78, 81, 111
Scott, Samuel, 84
Scottish Airways, 95
Seaham Harbour Company, 14
Secret Garden, The, 75
Sedgwick, Professor Adam, 17
Sennar Dam, 11, 51, 68
sewers, 11
Seymour, Lord Henry, 84
Seymour, James, 81, 82
Seymour family, 84
Sheffield, 11

Shell Oil Company, see Royal Dutch Shell
Sherwood, Lord, 106
Shetland, 95
Short Bros., 93
Sicily, 105
Sidmore, S. A., 103
Sidney, Sir Philip, 81
Simmonds Aircraft Ltd., 92, 93
Sinclair, Sir Archibald (Lord Thurso), 101, 105
Singer Building (New York), 56
Singleton, H., 84
Smiley, Major Michael, CVO, (son-in-law), 47, 76, 86, 112, 117, 126; Miranda, 111–12, 115, 127–8. See also Pearson, Lavinia
Smith, Logan Pearsall, 75
Snyders, Frans, 81
Société Générale Hellénique, 118
Solander, Daniel, 87
Somerset, 68
Somerset, Lord Charles, 84
Sotheby's, 108, 109
South Africa, 100
South Wales Electric Power, 54
Southern Countries' Agricultural Society, 126
Southern Railway, 93, 94, 104, 117
Southwell, Harriet Anne, 82
Spain, 69, 92
Spartan Aircraft, 93
Spencer-Churchill, Hon. Beryl (aunt), 17; family, 87
Spender, J. A., 20, 23, 24
Standard Oil, 20, 24, 52
steeplechasing, 17, 18
Stockholm, 96, 100
Storrington, 33
Streetes, Guilim, 84
Stuart, Princess Louisa Maria Teresa, 86
Stubbs, George, 87
Studleigh Agricultural College, 76
Sudan, 11, 51
Surrenden, 82
Surrey Commercial Dock, 14
Surtees, Robert, 75

Surveyors' Club, 57
Sussex Yeomanry, 18, 25, 26
Sylvester, Master and Miss, 83
Syria, 101

Tahiti, 83
Tampico, oilfield, 22; electricity, 53
Tangye, Nigel, 98
Taylor, A. J. P., 100
Tedder Plan, 102
Tehuantepec Railway, 11, 14, 17, 23, 53, 94
Tennant, Diana, 128
Texas, 22, 66, 67, 94
Thorneycroft, Hamo, 30
Thorpeness, 29, 78
Those in Authority, 16
Times, The, 40, 59, 110
Tocornal, Don Ismael, 55
Tonkin, Don Juan, 55–8, 63
Torres, Don Pedro, 55, 64
Townsend, Lady Charlotte, 38
trains, 11, 14, 17, 23, 53, 94; model, 94
Tramarie, Dr Pierre L'Espagnol de la, 52
trams, 53, 54, 55, 58
Transatlantic Ferry Service Pool, 101
Treasure Houses of Britain exhibition, 85
tree-planting, 49, 126
Trinidad, 65
Trinity College (Cambridge), 17
Tritton, Patrick ('Paddy', son-in-law), 77–8, 125, 126, 128; Judy, 78. *See also* Pearson, Veronica
Trivia, 75
Troy, François de, 86
Triumph of Louis XIII and His Wife, The, 87
Tuxpam oilfield, 22
Tuxpango Calcium Nitrate Plant, 23
Tuxpango Falls hydro-electric station, 23
Typos, 70

United Airways, 94

Valparaiso, 51, 53, 54, 61; Port, 56
Valparaiso Tramway Company, 54
Van der Gucht, Gerard, 86
Vandyck, Sir Anthony, 81, 86, 116
Van Somer, Paul, 82, 85, 86
vegetables, 111–3
Velasco House, 62
Venice, 85, 128
Vera Cruz, 24
Vera Cruz harbour, 17
Vera Cruz Light and Power Co., 23, 53
Vera Cruz oilfield, 21, 22
Verelst, Simon, 86
Vicars Bros., 82
Vichy, 94
visitors (to Parham), notes for guides, 120–3; numbers, 127
Vithek, Mr, 71

Wall Street, 13, 92
Wall Street Journal, The, 11
Walch, A. C., 64
Walsingham, Sir Francis, 37
Ward, Lady, 107
Wars, Pacific (Chile, Peru, Bolivia), 55; Spanish Civil, 69; First World War, 26, 93; Second World War, 12, 48–9, 105, 107, 116
Warsaw, 95
Washington D.C., 85
Waters Pierce Oil Co., 20, 21
waterworks, 14
Waugh, Evelyn, 72–3
Wavell, Lady, 109
Wentworth, Lady, 125, 126
Wessex Electricity Co., 55
West Africa, 94, 100
West of England Electric Investments, 55
Westminster, Abbot of, 36
Westminster Gazette, 20
Westminster Press, 35, 116
Westonbirt School, 78
Whitby, 84
White, Messrs J. G., 53, 56
White Papers, 106
Whitehall Electric Co., 23, 28, 53, 54, 68, 69, 74, 118

Whitehall Petroleum Company, 66
Whitehall Securities, 53, 55, 63, 64, 65, 66, 69, 77, 93, 94, 96, 103, 118
Williams-Ellis, Clough, 57
Wind in The Willows, The, 75
Wissing, Willem, 86
Wood, Sir Kingsley, 96, 100
Woolf, Miss, 75
Wootton, John, 81
Worswick, A. E., 60, 62
Wright, John Michael, 84

Wyndham, William, Lord Greville, 90

York, Cardinal, 86
York, Duchess of, 86
Young, Desmond, 11, 13
Young Pretender, The, 86

Zoffany, Johann, 83, 84
Zouche, Cecil, 38; Lady, 32, 35, 38, 81, 86, 90; Lord, 41, 82, 90, 115, 126
Zuccaro, Tadeo, 86